JERRY SAVELLE

What I Learned
from the men who imparted into me the most

Published by Jerry Savelle Ministries International
Crowley, Texas, U.S.A.
www.JerrySavelle.org

Unless otherwise noted, Scripture quotations are taken from the New King James Version ®. Copyright © 1982 by Thomas Nelson, Inc. Used by permission. All rights reserved.
KJV — King James Version. Authorized King James Version.
NIV — THE HOLY BIBLE, NEW INTERNATIONAL VERSION®, NIV® Copyright © 1973, 1978, 1984, 2011 by Biblica, Inc.® Used by permission. All rights reserved worldwide.
AMP — THE AMPLIFIED BIBLE, Old Testament copyright © 1965, 1987 by the Zondervan Corporation. The Amplified New Testament copyright © 1958, 1987 by the Lockman Foundation. Used by permission.

© 2014 Jerry Savelle Ministries International
All rights reserved.

ISBN 978-1-939934-07-9

Rights for publishing this book outside the U.S.A or in non-English languages are administered by Jerry Savelle Ministries International, an international not-for-profit ministry. For additional information, please visit JerrySavelle.org, or email info@jsmi.org, or write to
Jerry Savelle Ministries International, PO Box 748, Crowley, TX 76036, U.S.A.

To order copies of this book and other resources in bulk quantities,
please contact us at 1-817-297-3155.

Table of Contents

1	God's Call on My Life	1
2	Learning from Kenneth Copeland	11
3	Working with Kenneth Copeland	21
4	Kenneth E. Hagin	39
5	Oral Roberts	53
6	T.L. Osborn	73
7	Harold Nichols	85
8	Dave Malkin	89
	Photo Gallery	93
	A Conversation with Jerry and Carolyn Savelle	105

1

God's Call on My Life

I had looked forward to Thanksgiving for weeks, and when the big day arrived, I couldn't have been more excited. The year was 1957, and I would be celebrating my eleventh birthday in less than a month. Our entire family was gathered for a holiday reunion at my grandmother's home in Oklahoma City. Seeing everyone together made me forget about the long drive I'd just made all the way from Shreveport in the back seat of my parents' car.

November in Oklahoma is typically marked by sunny days, coupled with brisk temperatures and lots of wind—nothing that would deter a tenacious group of preteen boys from embarking on a full day of outdoor adventures while the turkey roasted in the oven. And that's just how my two cousins Joe McCroskey and Donnie Porter and I filled the hours until we heard Grandma declare the three most awaited words of the day: time to eat!

At last—we could eat Thanksgiving turkey and all the fixings until we popped.

I don't recall exactly how many family members were there; I just remember we were all crowded into my grandmother's little house. Some squeezed together at the table, others gathered on the porch outside, and some were just standing here and there with plates of food in hand.

Joe, Donnie, and I found a place to stand and eat in the living room, just as someone turned on the television. It took awhile for the old black-and-white set with the rabbit ears to come to life, but when the image became clear, we saw a tall man with dark hair speaking to a large group of people seated in rows of chairs beneath a big tent. By the looks on their faces, they were hanging on his every word.

I'd never seen the man before, but all of my Oklahoma relatives knew exactly who he was. "That's Oral Roberts," I heard one of them say. "Wait until he prays. You'll see people receive miracles right before your very eyes."

He was preaching a sermon entitled "The Fourth Man," which would later be recognized as one of his most famous tent sermons. As I stood there watching and listening, I was so captivated by what he said that I completely forgot about the plate of food in my hand.

When Roberts finished preaching, he sat down in a chair near the edge of the stage so that he could pray for the people who had lined up to experience God's healing touch. One by one, as they came forward for prayer, people were indeed healed from all sorts of diseases and conditions—and some even got out of their wheelchairs. I'd never seen anything like it in all of my ten years.

"Oral Roberts is a phony!" I heard one of my adult relatives say. "He pays people to get out of those wheelchairs—that's all fake." And yet, somehow I knew deep inside that what I'd just witnessed was as real as I was.

At that exact instant I heard these words: "Someday you'll preach like that. Someday you'll pray like that for people." At first I thought either Joe or Donnie was speaking to me, but when I turned to look at them, they were gone. I don't know how long I'd been standing there alone.

That's when I realized I'd just heard the voice of God, and it frightened me. I'd never heard God speak before, but at the age of ten I knew I had a call of God on my life. The problem was, being a preacher was not what I wanted to do; my dream was to own my own paint and body shop. I remember thinking, if I never tell anybody about what I just heard, then eventually God will realize He made a mistake and will call on somebody who really wants to do this. Not me.

So I never told anyone what happened that Thanksgiving in my grandmother's living room. I didn't tell my cousins. I didn't tell my parents. And I certainly didn't tell the pastor of the little Baptist church we attended in Shreveport, even when he came to our house as he was accustomed to doing from time to time. He was one of those pastors who, if you even sneezed, knew about it and was at your house immediately to pray for you. But my lips were sealed. I was certain that my secret was safe and my future plans to own my own business were secure.

I had no idea that Thanksgiving Day 1957 had inalterably marked my life.

Running from God

I carried on with my life: went to school, played ball, and applied myself to learning everything I could about cars. After I finished school, it wasn't all that long before I achieved my dream of operating my own paint and body shop.

When Carolyn and I married in 1966, she already knew I had the call of God on my life, though she'd never heard me talk about it. But she prayed for me.

Carolyn had grown up in a Pentecostal church, and she was familiar with the ministries of Oral Roberts, A. A. Allen, Jack Cole, and William Branham, God's powerful men of that generation. She was accustomed to attending numerous meetings and revivals, and after we were married, in hopes I would surrender to the call of God on my life, she always wanted me to attend with her.

But when you are running from God like I was, Satan will see to it that you are introduced to the kind of preachers who will make a wrong impression on you. At most of the meetings Carolyn and I attended together, the preachers did nothing that impressed me in a positive way. To me, the way they told sad stories and begged for money made them look like a bunch of wimps. What's more, I observed that some of them were not men of integrity, even though they were preachers. Don't get me wrong: I knew I was a sinner, but at least I considered myself an honest sinner.

My dad and my grandfather had taught me the importance of integrity and of keeping my word. I grew up in an era where people didn't require the help of a lawyer to draw up an agreement. For people of integrity, a handshake was the same as a binding contract. And that's how I ran my business. Occasionally I would give someone a quote to repair their car, and once I got into the job, I'd find the repair work was going to be more involved and cost more than I'd originally thought. But since I considered my handshake a binding contract, I always kept my word and charged only the agreed-upon amount.

I didn't see a lot of that kind of integrity in ministry during those days. My attitude was this: if you had to lie, manipulate, and play on people's emotions to be a preacher, then I didn't want any part of it. It seemed the devil kept running preachers like that across my path, which in my mind was a perfectly good reason not to surrender to the ministry call I knew was on my life.

I was tired of going to church with Carolyn and listening to sad stories told by preachers who begged for money and always tried to talk me out of my hard-earned cash. I remember thinking, why don't they get a real job? As far as I could tell, all they did was eat, sleep, and preach.

Carolyn would occasionally invite one of them to our house. It seemed to me that all preachers loved to eat chicken, and my wife was always happy to fry some for them. I, however, remained convinced that all they really wanted was my money—and my chicken.

In 1969, a preacher from Texas came to Shreveport and conducted a one-week series of services. Carolyn went to every service, and each day when I came home from my shop, dressed in my Jerry's Paint & Body Shop uniform and covered in grease and bondo dust from head-to-toe, she would beg me to go with her to the evening service. Each time she asked, I told her I was tired and didn't want to go hear yet another preacher tell sad stories and beg for money.

Finally, on the last night of the services, Carolyn said, "Jerry, this is the final night he will be here. I promise you, he's not like all the rest. If you go with me tonight and it turns out you don't like him, I'll never ask you to go to another meeting."

I thought, well, that's just the deal I've been waiting for. And so I went, expecting to return home with my free ticket out of church—forever.

But as it turned out, Carolyn was right. This guy wasn't like the others. There were certain things he said and did in that service that really got my attention—just as Oral Roberts had gotten my attention back in 1957.

I watched the young preacher from Texas walk up to the pulpit with such boldness and confidence that it was as if John Wayne himself had just ridden into town. This preacher didn't tell sad stories. He didn't cry. He didn't beg for money. He just confidently laid out the Word of God, line upon line, in a way that was both compelling and easy to understand. I felt like he was talking just to me.

I'll never forget his closing remarks: "If you believe what the Bible says, it will work for you. If you don't believe it, it won't. Good night."

I thought, wow—I've never seen a preacher like this before. This is the kind of preacher I've been waiting for!

The Most Important Decision of My Life

I didn't surrender to the call of God that night like Carolyn had hoped, but when I got to my shop the next day, I couldn't get the things I'd seen and heard the night before out of my mind.

A couple of guys who worked for me were finishing work on the cars that were to be ready at the end of the day. You can imagine their surprise when I told them we weren't going to do any more work that day, and they should go home.

"What about these cars?" they asked. I said I'd call the owners and tell them to come tomorrow. The men left, and then I shut the overhead doors and locked the office door. Once I was certain I was alone, I began to look for the Bible Carolyn had given me the day I opened my business. I'd hidden it so that my customers wouldn't see it, and it took awhile before I found it under a stack of my paint catalogs.

I took the Bible with me into the shop restroom and locked the door. As a matter of fact, I'd locked every door in the building. I wanted to be sure no one knew what I was doing as I sat on the floor and read the scriptures the preacher had talked about the night before. I cried like a baby as I read God's promises for myself. I was fully aware that I couldn't run from Him—or His call upon my life—any longer.

When I got home after work, I didn't say anything to Carolyn about what had happened to me that day. We went to bed at the usual time, but I couldn't sleep. Finally, at about three o'clock in the morning, I got the Bible and took it into our living room where I laid on the sofa and read the scriptures again. This time the words moved beyond my mind and settled deep within my spirit. After a while, I stood up, lifted my hands, and said, "God, I don't know why You would want me. I've been running from You all my life, but if You still want me, here I am."

That's when the presence of God came into the room. I don't know how to describe it other than I felt as though I were standing outside at midday and the sun was shining on no one else but me. I realized tears were running down my face.

The next thing I knew, I began to pray in the Holy Ghost. I stood there with my hands uplifted, praying out loud until almost seven o'clock in the morning. The experience had lasted four hours.

I thought I was alone in the room, but when I turned around, I was surprised to see both Carolyn and her mother sitting on the sofa—and both were crying. I looked at Carolyn and said, "Guess what happened to me?"

"We know," she replied.

"How do you know?"

"I heard a noise in the living room last night, and when I realized you weren't in the bed, I got up to find out what was going on. When I saw you standing there, I called Mama and said, 'You've got to come over here and see what's happening to Jerry.'"

I kissed Carolyn, told her I loved her, and then I asked her to forgive me for being such an idiot and running from God. Then I walked over to my mother-in-law, who'd also been praying for me for a long time, and I kissed her and told her I loved her too. I'd never done that before, and that's when I knew my experience in the presence of God was really real. I no longer had a mother-in-law; I had another mama. Mary Creech has been a great asset to my life and ministry for more than forty years now, and I thank God for her.

My life changed that night in February 1969. I was immediately consumed by the desire to fulfill God's call on my life—but I had no idea where to start. Obviously the preacher from Texas had already left town, yet I had an overwhelming desire to hear more of his messages. I just didn't know how to make it happen.

A couple of weeks later, a friend of Carolyn's who had attended all of the services that week in February came to our house. She had a brown-paper grocery bag filled with reel-to-reel audiotapes that had been recorded at the meetings. She said, "Jerry, the Lord told me to bring you these tapes."

"What am I supposed to do with them? I don't have any way to listen to them," I said.

"You don't have a tape player?"

"No, I don't."

She said, "I'll be right back," and then she went home and brought back a tape player. It was huge and had two big speakers attached to it. "I was hoping you had one, but God told me to bring this one to you. I'm giving you both the tapes and the tape player," she said.

I set up that tape player in our little guest bedroom, which had now become my office, and I took those reel-to-reel tapes and started listening to them. My hunger to learn was insatiable; I couldn't get enough of God's Word. I listened to those tapes every spare moment I had until the Lord spoke to me and instructed me to shut down my business and spend no less than eight hours each day studying His Word for the next three months. And that's just what I did.

God used those tapes as my introduction to the Bible. He also used them as my introduction to a man named Kenneth Copeland, that young preacher from Texas whom God used to impact my life more significantly than anyone else I've known.

Impact and Impartation

Although I didn't realize it at the time, God had already used two men I'd never even met—Oral Roberts and Kenneth Copeland—to impact my life. He used Oral Roberts in 1957 to establish His call on my life, and twelve years later He used Kenneth Copeland to help establish me in His Word.

In the years that followed, God used others to help as He molded my heart and forged my faith. I learned valuable truths from men like Kenneth Hagin, T.L. Osborn, Harold Nichols, and Dave Malkin. Some of these names are well known; others are not. But the common thread that ties these men together is they were each used in a significant way, not only to impact my life, but also to impart some aspect of what God had given to them into me.

By the time I was twenty-three years old, I was living the life I'd dreamed of since childhood: I owned my own paint and body shop, I was married to a godly woman, and we had two beautiful daughters. If someone had told me at that time I would close my dream business and become the founder of what would one day be an international ministry with offices on four continents, I would have thought they were out of their mind. And yet, I'd never forgotten those two simple sentences the Spirit of God spoke to me in 1957 as I watched Oral Roberts for the first time: "Someday you'll preach like that. Someday you'll pray like that."

I will never regret answering God's call on my life.

If you are reading this book, it stands to reason there is a call of God on your life. Perhaps you too are called to preach and to pray like I was. Your call may be to pastor a church, teach God's Word, or be an evangelist. The call of God, however, is not restricted to what many refer to as full-time ministry. God may call you to the marketplace, to fill a role in government, or to minister to those in your own home. Regardless of where God places you, He wants you to be empowered to carry out your assignment effectively and fulfill His call upon your life.

That's why I've written this book just for you. With the exception of Kenneth Copeland and myself, the men I will be talking about have all finished their earthly work and gone to be with the Lord. And yet, the words they spoke and the impact they had on my life and the lives of thousands of people throughout the world are still as active and

What I Learned *from the men who imparted into me the most*

anointed as ever.

By sharing the wisdom and insight I gained from each of these men with you, I believe your own life and ministry will be impacted no less significantly than mine was. But more, I also believe you will receive an impartation of anointing commensurate with the unique call of God on your own life.

I encourage you to put God first in every area of your life and to always count it an honor that He has called you, anointed you, and believes in you.

2

Learning from Kenneth Copeland

I had come in contact with a lot of preachers before I first saw Kenneth Copeland in 1969, but none of the others came across like Copeland did. Looking back, I realize the four things that attracted me to him were his boldness, his confidence in God, his integrity, and his refusal to compromise.

Rather than pleading for money like other preachers did, he boldly stated that God was his source and God supplied all of his needs. Brother Copeland refused to use gimmicks to play on the people's emotions, and that impressed me in a positive way. Manipulation was not his style. I realized it had been what I call the "religious cons" that had made me not want to be a preacher. But after watching Copeland, I felt I'd found a preacher I could trust—and I wanted to be like him.

I've since learned that when you're called to preach, it's important to find someone else to hold as an example of what you want to be like. For me, that person was Kenneth Copeland. Back then, not everyone was as excited about his bold message as I was. Some people even tried to discourage me from listening to him. I remember one man said to me, "He's an extremist."

"What's an extremist?" I asked.

"Well, he doesn't preach the whole counsel of God. He just focuses on one thing, and there is so much more in the Bible."

I knew this man meant well, so I made a point to listen to Kenneth Copeland a little closer. As it turned out, I discovered the man was right. Copeland *was* an extremist. He was extremely blessed, extremely prosperous, and extremely positive. I remember thinking, I want to be an extremist too! And with that decision, Kenneth Copeland became my mentor.

A lot of people think a mentor is someone you spend personal time with and receive instruction from, day in and day out. This is not always true. In my case, Kenneth Copeland became my mentor from afar as he tutored me daily through his teachings.

He didn't have any books at that time. All I had access to were his big reel-to-reel taped messages, which I listened to constantly. I dissected them. I made written outlines of each message so that I could study them over and over. That is how he mentored me.

The more I listened to his messages, the more impressed I was with his delivery of the Word of God, his lifestyle, his behavior, and the way he conducted his ministry. This man's words made God seem so very real. The way he demonstrated how Christians could actually live by the Word of God in total freedom made the victorious Christian lifestyle something I wanted for myself and for my family.

The more I studied God's Word, the more I saw how obvious it was that God wants us to be winners, because if we are winners, then it makes the God we serve more attractive to those who are lost.

All of a sudden, the Bible Carolyn had given me was no longer a big, old black book filled with stories of people who'd lived thousands of years ago. *It was the living Word of God.* I'll never forget the first time I held that Bible against my chest as I walked into that little bedroom where I studied, and I declared, "This is the Word of God. This is God talking to Jerry Savelle. I am what the Bible says I am."

I'd heard Brother Copeland say, "You are what He says you are. You have what He says you have. You can do what He says you can do, and you can be what He says you can be." So, throughout the day, I would walk the floor, holding my Bible to my chest and quoting Brother Copeland. As a result, for the first time in my life the Bible took on a new meaning for me—it was now the integrity of God; it was His bond.

I remember something else Brother Copeland said that made an impact on me in those days: "When you get to the place in your life where you believe the Bible just like you believe the word of your doctor, your lawyer, or your very best friend, your life will never be the same." Now, there was a time when you could believe your doctor. You could believe your lawyer, and you could believe your very best friend. I'm not so sure this is always true these days, but there was a time when people didn't think twice about believing those with whom they had trusting relationships. So I knew what Brother Copeland meant about believing the Bible.

I learned that when you get to the place where God's Word is the final authority in all you do, your life will never be the same.

Integrity and Authority

One of the initial truths I learned from Kenneth Copeland's messages was the absolute integrity of God's Word. Once that fact was established in my life, I learned how vital it was to give the Word of God first place each day and to make it the final authority in every situation.

I'd never before considered the Bible as God's integrity, but it made sense when I saw these words God had spoken: "My covenant I will not break, nor alter the word that has gone out of My lips" (Psalm 89:34).

When Brother Copeland taught about the authority of God's Word, he consistently used two particular scripture references to illustrate his message. The first was Matthew 8:5–13:

> Now when Jesus had entered Capernaum, a centurion came to Him, pleading with Him, saying, "Lord, my servant is lying at home paralyzed, dreadfully tormented."
> And Jesus said to him, "I will come and heal him."
> The centurion answered and said, "Lord, I am not worthy that You should come under my roof. But only speak a word, and my servant will be healed. For I also am a man under authority, having soldiers under me. And I say to this one, 'Go,' and he goes; and to another, 'Come,' and he comes; and to my servant, 'Do this,' and he does it."
> When Jesus heard it, He marveled, and said to those who followed, "Assuredly, I say to you, I have not found such great faith, not even in Israel! And I say to you that many will come from east and west, and sit down with Abraham, Isaac, and Jacob in the kingdom of heaven. But the sons of the kingdom will be cast out into outer darkness. There will be weeping and gnashing of teeth." Then Jesus said to the centurion, "Go your way; and as you have believed, so let it be done for you." And his servant was healed that same hour.

Brother Copeland would read this passage, and then he would say, "When you get to the place where all you need is God's Word and nothing else, then God will marvel at your faith, and you will have what the Bible refers to as the greatest faith." Those words made a big impression on me. I wanted to get to the place in my life where all I needed was what God had to say. This desire helped Carolyn and me get to the place where—no matter what we were going through—our first thought was, what does the Word say? Before we would ever pray about a matter, we would make it a point to find out what God's Word says, and then we would build our prayer based on the truth we'd found.

That's how we gave God's Word first place in our lives and made it the final authority.

The other scripture reference Brother Copeland used was Luke 10:38–42:

> Now it happened as they went that He entered a certain village; and a certain woman named Martha welcomed Him into her house. And she had a sister called Mary, who also sat at Jesus' feet and heard His word. But Martha was distracted with much serving, and she approached Him and said, "Lord, do You not care that my sister has left me to serve alone? Therefore tell her to help me."
>
> And Jesus answered and said to her, "Martha, Martha, you are worried and troubled about many things. But one thing is needed, and Mary has chosen that good part, which will not be taken away from her."

When Brother Copeland taught on the integrity of God's Word, the phrase from the above scripture he would always emphasize was "one thing is needed." He'd say, "Whatever the Word says, that's final authority." Carolyn and I learned from Brother Copeland how to find out what the Word says, make it the final authority, and then refuse to compromise. This is how we've lived our lives for the past forty-five years, and I can tell you that doing so works.

Walking by Faith

The next foundational truth I learned from Brother Copeland's messages was how to walk by faith. I'd heard other preachers claim they were living by faith, but if their lives were an example of what living by faith was like, I wasn't impressed. Based on what I saw, it seemed to me that living by faith meant you never knew what God was going to do.

The living by faith concept other preachers talked about made a defeated lifestyle sound normal. I once heard a woman say of one of these preachers, "Oh, that poor man. He has nobody to trust but God." I remember thinking, who else do you need? But when Brother Copeland talked about living by faith, it was in the context of living in total victory: "Faith is the method of overcoming the world; the just shall live by faith; it is impossible to please God without faith."

All I knew was, I wanted to learn how to live by faith the way Brother Copeland did, and I couldn't get enough of his teaching.

I was listening to a new set of his reel-to-reel tapes one day when I heard him say for the first time, "I'm not moved by what I see. I'm not moved by what I hear. I'm not moved by what I feel. I'm only moved by what I believe, and I believe the Word of God." I didn't realize it at the time, but he was quoting Smith Wigglesworth, a British evangelist who'd become known as "the apostle of faith" before he died in 1947. Apparently Brother Copeland had studied Wigglesworth's messages as intently as I was now studying Copeland's messages.

When Brother Copeland said he was not moved by what he saw, what he heard, or what he felt, I thought, well . . . I am! How can you *not* be moved by what you see, what you hear, and what you feel? It's common knowledge that seeing is believing, right? That's the way we've all been raised and taught, and yet here's Brother Copeland with this totally foreign concept that says we're not to be moved by these things.

Although I didn't know how to make it happen, my immediate quest was to be in a place where I was no longer moved by my five physical senses. I wanted to be moved only by the Word of God.

I remember I did a lot of walking back and forth in that little bedroom office I'd created, repeating exactly what Brother Copeland had said: "I am not moved by what I see. I am not moved by what I hear. I am not moved by what I feel. I'm only moved by what I believe—and I believe the Word of God." I would say this over and over, day after day after day, never quite convinced it was true. But I kept at it, and after a period of time, what I was saying took root. I was no longer quoting Kenneth Copeland; I was making a faith declaration that had just become a way of life for me. And it remains a way of life for Carolyn and me, our children, and our grandchildren to this day.

Standing in Faith

As previously mentioned, when we began our life of faith, our family included two beautiful little girls, Jerriann and Terri.

We continued to listen to any of Kenneth Copeland's tapes we could get our hands on, and you can imagine how excited we were to learn he would be returning to our church for a second time to conduct a series of meetings. We arranged our schedules so that we could attend every one of the services, and signed the girls up for the childcare the church provided. We knew the upcoming week would be life changing.

What we didn't know was our faith in God's Word was about to be tested beyond anything we could imagine.

One morning as we were listening to Brother Copeland conclude his message, we heard the unmistakable sound of our toddler, Terri, screaming at the top of her voice as she was being carried into the auditorium by one of the nursery workers. Both Terri and the nursery worker were covered with blood that was pouring from Terri's hand.

As I took Terri in my arms, I thought, okay—now we're going to find out if I really believe this stuff. I also knew we were going to find out if Kenneth Copeland believed it. After all, it happened during his service.

I was holding my daughter as I turned to look at Brother Copeland to see how he was going to react. If he had jumped up and said, "Oh my God! Why did this have to happen to me? I was almost done, almost out of here," both my faith and my confidence in him would have been destroyed. But that's not what happened.

He simply said, "Bring her to me." And so I did.

He laid his hands on Terri and said, "In the name of Jesus, I command this pain to stop and the bleeding to cease."

Terri stopped crying, and at the same time, the bleeding stopped. She laid her head on my shoulder and closed her eyes. It was as simple as that.

As I walked out of the auditorium, I heard Brother Copeland say to everyone who had just witnessed what happened, "Now, I'm not through preaching. Let's get back in the Word." Despite the fact that some of the people were still in panic mode, Brother Copeland continued like it was just another routine day in the life of Kenneth Copeland. He got right back up and continued preaching from the fourth chapter of Mark. He'd been teaching us that once the Word is sown, Satan comes immediately to steal it. I heard him say, "We just had a prime example of this."

I took Terri into the men's restroom to wash the blood from her hand, and that's when I saw the source of the blood: two of her little fingertips had been completely severed. Just then there was a knock at the door, and the nursery attendant asked if she could come in. I said yes.

"Brother Jerry, I found these on the floor and I didn't know what to do with them," she said as she placed two little fingertips with the nails still on them into my hand. They had been severed when Terri crawled behind a moving rocking chair.

At that moment I had to make a decision: was I going to forget everything I'd learned over the past months and be moved by what I could very plainly see was real, or was I going to take a stand on the Word of God and exercise my faith? That's the day I realized all of my confessing God's Word over and over again had taken root. I looked at those little fingertips as I opened my Bible, and with Terri still in my arms, I said out loud, "Father, I am not moved by what I see."

I turned to Deuteronomy 28 where it said the fruit of my body would be blessed, and I said, "God, this little girl is the fruit of my body." I turned to Galatians 3 where it said Abraham's blessings are mine, and I said, "I am a covenant man. I'm entitled to the blessings of Abraham." Finally, I turned to Mark 11 where it said I could have whatever I said if I would believe in my heart and not doubt, and I declared, "My God will restore my baby's fingers!"

I wrapped the fingertips in a piece of tissue and put them in my pocket. Then I took Terri back into the auditorium where Carolyn had remained seated, I sat down, and I finished listening to Brother Copeland's message. That's when I knew with certainty I'd reached the place I longed to be, the place where I was not moved by my five physical senses.

I'd just become a marked man.

Of course, we took Terri to a specialist who performed a skin graph and then carefully dressed the fingers. He told us in no uncertain terms that although he'd done all he could do, Terri's fingers would never be normal. We listened politely to what he said, but Carolyn and I refused to accept it.

We had learned to put the Word first place in our lives. We had learned to make the Word final authority in every situation. We had developed in our revelation of God's integrity. We were no longer moved by what we saw, what we heard, or what we felt.

For the next few days we went on with our lives, standing on the Word of God. We continued to confess God's Word over our daughter's fingers, and we thanked Him for healing her.

When Carolyn and I took Terri back to the surgeon a few days later for a follow-up examination, we were unwavering in our faith that God would restore our daughter's fingertips. The doctor who treated Terri was an Asian man who served Buddha; he even had a number of statues throughout his office. But we were not moved by what we saw. We remained focused on our God and the healing that had already been provided through Jesus Christ.

The doctor greeted us when he entered the room, and then he turned his attention to Terri. Carolyn and I watched quietly as he removed the dressing from Terri's fingers. Suddenly he stepped back, lifted both hands, and screamed *my God* as he gazed at the most beautiful little pink fingers, totally restored, with perfectly positioned little fingernails.

I said, "No, sir, not your god—*my* God!"

Carolyn and I have shared this testimony many times over the years as an encouragement to others to stand in faith on God's Word, regardless of what their five senses may tell them. It has been such a blessing when people write and tell us they also have had situations with their own children that required them to stand on God's Word. And in each instance, God moved in the same miraculous way for them as He did for Terri.

When I look back to those days I spent listening to tapes over and over again in that little bedroom I'd converted to my study office, I thank God for Kenneth Copeland and his boldness to teach others how to be moved by nothing but the Word of God.

3

Working with Kenneth Copeland

When Kenneth Copeland returned to Shreveport for another meeting at our church, Life Tabernacle, his wife, Gloria, was with him. As was customary at the time, they were guests in the home of one of the couples who attended the church. That couple just happened to be Carolyn's parents, Olen and Mary Creech.

It was Olen who first introduced me to Brother Copeland, and through our newfound friendship he heard the rest of the story about Terri's fingers and learned that because of my being inspired by what I'd learned from listening to his tapes I'd stepped out into ministry.

I had no idea at the time that meeting the man who had been mentoring me through his taped messages was about to change the course of my life yet again.

Later that week, during one of the evening services, Brother Copeland stopped in the middle of his message and asked me to stand up. He said, "Jerry, God showed me in prayer today that you and I will be a team someday. We will spend the rest of our lives preaching the Word of God together around the world." He paused for a moment and then added, "It will be your responsibility to believe God for the perfect timing for the team to begin."

You can imagine how thrilled I was to hear this word coming from the man who had been mentoring me through his tapes, day in and day out, since the first time I saw him. And now my mentor had just declared publicly that God told him we would be a team. I was both overwhelmed and honored by his words.

You can probably also imagine that not everyone in the service was thrilled to hear Kenneth Copeland and I were going to be a team. I remembered the warnings I'd been given when he first came to our church. "He's an extremist," I'd been told. Well, now I was an extremist too. I was also blessed, highly favored, and fortunate.

I began seeking God in earnest regarding His timing for the team to begin. I knew I had to have an outlet for the Word that I was consistently pouring into my spirit, so I had been preaching in the streets, sharing what I was learning with people on a one-on-one basis. God was developing within me a new kind of love for people (His love), and along with this love came a strong desire to win souls. There were times when I would go out and win as many as a hundred people to the Lord.

As I continued to study Brother Copeland's messages, I sensed a similarity between his ministry and what I would be doing. I knew I would become a teacher of the Word like he was, but that didn't mean I would lose my love for seeing people come to Christ through one-on-one evangelism. During this season of soul winning, God was adding the office of teacher to my ministry.

I was out preaching in the streets, and I would occasionally preach in a home Bible study or at a youth meeting, taking what I'd learned from Brother Copeland to those who crossed my path at God's direction. In 1970, about nine months following the time when Brother Copeland spoke the prophetic word over me, I was conducting one of these youth meetings at a church in Oklahoma City. I remember praying before I left that my old car would make it to Oklahoma City and back. We began with the twenty young people who attended the church, and in a week's time we had won more than eighty teenagers to the Lord. It was a great meeting.

While I was in Oklahoma City, Brother Copeland called our home in Shreveport and talked to Carolyn. He asked where I was, and she told him Oklahoma City. He said, "As soon as he gets home, tell him I need him to be with me in Florida at Jacksonville Beach."

My old Oldsmobile got me back to Shreveport, just as I'd prayed, and then we loaded it up again for the drive to Jacksonville. But this time it wasn't just me traveling. There was also Carolyn, her mother, and our two young daughters.

Each time we got in the car, we prayed and believed for it to start, and then later we'd pray for it to stop when it was supposed to. The engine was bad and so were the brakes! We got as far as Montgomery, Alabama, and the fuel pump went out. I bought another fuel pump and put it on the car, which enabled us to get all the way to Florida.

When we got to Jacksonville, Brother Copeland said, "I'm going to preach three services today, and I want you to watch me. But between those services, I want you to go out on the beach and witness like you do."

While we were in Jacksonville Beach, I witnessed to people one-on-one, and nearly 150 came to Christ right out on the beach. Many of those people then came to Brother Copeland's service, where he taught them the Word and got them filled with the Holy Ghost. It was an exciting time for me and my family.

One afternoon Brother Copeland asked if I'd been praying about when the team would begin.

"Yes, sir," I said.

"When are you coming to Fort Worth?" he asked. His ministry

What I Learned *from the men who imparted into me the most*

was located in Fort Worth, and I knew he wasn't asking when I was coming to visit. He wanted to know when Carolyn and I would be moving there.

Before I even had time to process his question, let alone talk to Carolyn, I heard these words come out of my mouth: "Just as soon as I get home, we'll leave and move to Fort Worth." And because Carolyn and I were in total agreement about the move, that's just what we did.

But something important happened the last day we were in Shreveport. We were at Carolyn's parents' house, and I went out to her dad's garden to pray. As I walked up and down the rows of fully grown cornstalks, thanking God for the opportunity He'd given me, the Spirit of God spoke this to me: "When you get to Fort Worth and begin traveling with Kenneth Copeland, you are to watch him like a hawk. There are three things I want to teach you."

I love the way God speaks to each of us with words and phrases that are meaningful to our individual temperament and upbringing. I'm a country boy, so I understood what God meant when He said to watch Brother Copeland like a hawk. Hawks have keen eyesight. They can spot even the slightest movement in a field from a great distance away. And yet I had the opportunity to watch Kenneth Copeland from close up.

I knew the next phase of my mentoring had just begun.

Two days after we settled into our new home in Fort Worth, Brother Copeland said, "We're leaving tomorrow and will be gone three weeks. You will drive the car and take the equipment. So now we begin as a team."

Our first meeting took place in Louisville, Kentucky, where I attended my first service as Brother Copeland's full-time employee. Just as God had instructed, I watched him like a hawk. I watched and listened as he delivered his messages at three services each day for a week. I watched everything he did. I watched how he ministered to people, how he prayed for them.

Most of the things I learned from Kenneth Copeland didn't come from his sitting down with me and saying, "Now, Jerry, this is what I want to teach you today," though there were a few cherished times when this happened. The greater part of what I learned from Brother Copeland came through observation. And as I observed him, the three things God spoke to me about when I was praying among the cornstalks in my father-in-law's garden became clear to me: number one, God would to teach me how to preach with authority; number two, He would teach me how to pray for the sick; and number three, He would to teach me how to tap into His wisdom.

Preaching with Authority

Traveling with Kenneth Copeland became my seminary. As a matter of fact, when he was conducting a service, I was oftentimes so locked into what he was saying as I sat with him on the platform that I forgot anyone else was there. On numerous occasions someone would approach me afterwards and say, "What were you so mad about while Brother Copeland was preaching?"

I'd say, "Mad? I wasn't mad about anything."

"Well, by the look on your face, it appeared to everyone that you were mad."

I explained that I wasn't mad; I was intent. (I just didn't mention that while I was once standing in a patch of corn, God had told me to watch Brother Copeland like a hawk.)

During those sessions, I wrote down everything he said. I kept a journal of the truths I was learning from him. When we were in the car together and I couldn't write down something he said, I'd immediately think to myself, I have the mind of Christ and I will remember every word.

Each time I watched and listened to Brother Copeland preach and minister to people, I would ask myself, how can someone be as bold and authoritative as he is? Is this something that can be learned? I knew God wanted me to preach with authority, so every day I would pour over the scriptures I'd heard him preach.

One day he was preaching from the book of Acts. Later in my hotel room, I was going over my notes when I read this scripture: "Now when they saw the boldness of Peter and John, and perceived that they were uneducated and untrained men, . . ." (Acts 4:13). In other words, here were these two men who were uneducated and untrained, yet they were preaching with boldness.

Okay, I thought, but how did they get to be so bold? Then I read the rest of the words in verse 13: ". . . they marveled. And they realized that they had been with Jesus." That phrase "they had been with Jesus" jumped from the page of my Bible right into my heart. "That's it!" I shouted. "Those men were bold because they had been with Jesus!"

Now I understood. The reason Brother Copeland was so bold and taught with such authority was that he spent time with Jesus before each service. Then I remembered something Brother Copeland taught me before we made our first trip together. He actually set it forth as a rule whenever he was preaching.

"When I come out of my hotel room for you to drive me to the meeting, don't talk to me," he said. Then he explained, "The last voice I want to hear before I preach is the voice of Jesus."

Brother Copeland continued, "After three o'clock, don't interrupt me—no matter what comes up. That's my time with Jesus; it's my prayer time. If you don't know how to set up the sound system, confess that you have the mind of Christ, and He will show you what to do. If you run into a problem, ask the Lord to help you solve it. He is faithful."

I always honored Brother Copeland's time with the Lord, and I could see the results of his commitment to that time.

The moment he stepped onto the platform after being with Jesus, the boldness, authority, and anointing that flowed from Brother Copeland was tangible. When he came out of his hotel room, it wasn't to play church; he had kingdom business to conduct. He didn't care what anyone thought. It didn't matter what the rules were at the church where he was speaking, what their denomination was, or what they believed or didn't believe. Kenneth Copeland taught the Word of God, line upon line and precept upon precept.

I would find out later that Brother Copeland had observed this process when he was working for Oral Roberts, serving as the co-pilot of his airplane and also as his driver when he went to meetings. Before meetings, no one spoke to Brother Roberts unless he first spoke to them—and that included his wife, Evelyn. Everyone understood the importance of his vital connection to Jesus, for out of that connection flowed the boldness, authority, and anointing that produced miracles.

As I sat in my hotel room and read Acts 13 again, I recalled the first time I'd seen Brother Copeland and how he had reminded me of John Wayne in the pulpit. And now I understood why: his boldness and authority came from spending time with Jesus.

I decided right then I would conduct my ministry the very same way. Brother Copeland's manner of conduct became my manner of conduct. Anyone who has traveled with me will tell you that, after three o'clock, I don't engage in anything but prayer and spending time with Jesus.

When we first launched out into our ministry, Carolyn and I would travel with our young girls. We couldn't afford two hotel rooms back then, so we all stayed together in one room until three o'clock each afternoon. That's when Carolyn would take the girls out to do something while I spent time with Jesus.

There were times when I would say, "You girls can come back into the room now." I would walk around the room with my hands behind my back, praying in the Holy Ghost before I went to preach.

Both girls would put their little hands behind their back like I did, and follow me around the room, also praying in the Holy Ghost. And then, once we returned to the room following the service, they'd always ask, "Daddy, can we feel your hands? They're always hot after you pray for people. Can we feel them?" Even at their tender ages, they recognized the anointing of God.

Spending time with Jesus has certainly paid off for me over the last four decades, just as it did for Oral Roberts and still does for Kenneth Copeland. Spending time with Jesus is the single most vital component of a ministry that is committed to preaching with authority.

Praying for the Sick

The second thing I learned while traveling with Brother Copeland was how to pray for the sick.

I was already comfortable praying for people and leading them to the Lord. What I didn't know was that praying for the sick was an entirely different matter—that is, if I wanted results. The thing I observed about Brother Copeland was that the anointing of God was always there when he got ready to pray for the sick. Again, this was a result of the time he'd spent with Jesus before his meetings.

There's an old saying that goes like this: "Miracles are not always the result of just good preaching; they are the result of good praying." In other words, good praying will bring on good preaching, and then the miracles will come.

As I watched Kenneth Copeland during those early days of our ministry together, I saw all kinds of miracles. I saw the crippled rise and walk. I saw the deaf receive their hearing. And I saw blind eyes opened. As a young minister just beginning my journey and wanting to be used by God, those miracles had a significant impact on me. I wanted to understand how Brother Copeland got those results.

I observed one thing in particular: He didn't just walk up and lay hands on people who needed healing. He never laid his hands on someone until he was ready to release his faith. Making that "point of contact" was something he'd learned from Oral Roberts.

Brother Copeland said to me, "While you are praying for someone who is sick, wait until your faith reaches its highest level, and then lay hands on them." After he told me this, I began watching him with new understanding as I waited for the moment he would lay his hands on someone. Time after time, he would pray over a person first, and then, when his faith was at its highest level, he would lay his hands on the person at what Brother Roberts had first called the point of contact.

Many times Brother Copeland would pray in the Holy Ghost before he would lay hands on someone. The Bible teaches that when we pray in the Holy Ghost, we build ourselves up in our most holy faith (see Jude 1:20). Brother Copeland knew that when he was praying for the sick, it was essential to wait until that faith was at its highest. Then when he knew it was time to release his faith, he transmitted it by the laying on of hands.

Knowing when to release faith requires continually listening to the Holy Ghost for instructions. This is another thing I observed while watching Brother Copeland pray for the sick: he listened to the Holy Ghost when he ministered to people, because that is how Jesus ministered to people.

Jesus said, "Most assuredly, I say to you, the Son can do nothing of Himself, but what He sees the Father do; for whatever He does, the Son also does in like manner" (John 5:19). Jesus didn't minister the same way in every situation. Sometimes He would lay hands on people and they were healed. Sometimes he just spoke the Word and they were healed. And other times people touched Him and they were healed.

One time when Jesus made a mixture of spittle and clay and placed it in the eye of a blind man, that man received his sight. Remember, Jesus said He only did what He'd seen the Father do. Apparently He'd seen His Father do that very thing when He first created mankind from dust, and Jesus reenacted it. There were times when He heard His Father say, "Lay your hands on them," and that's just what He did.

Just as Jesus watched and listened for His Father's instructions, so did Brother Copeland. He did this because a particular healing sometimes required more than the laying on of hands; it required an additional point of contact.

At times these additional points of contact were unusual. For instance, I once watched Brother Copeland minister to a man who had stomach cancer. Brother Copeland prayed until his faith reached its highest point, and then he laid his hands on the man. Then Brother Copeland stood there for a while not saying a word. All of a sudden ... bam! He hit the man in the stomach, knocking him to the floor. I thought, oh, dear God, he's killed that guy and we're both going to jail!

But then the man got up and declared, "I'm healed ... I'm healed!"

The next day the man returned and testified during the meeting. He said because he'd had stomach cancer, he'd been limited in what he could eat. But after Brother Copeland prayed for him, he'd gone to a Mexican restaurant and eaten a whole, big plateful of food. Then he said, "And I'm going back to that restaurant and doing the same thing tonight. I'm healed!"

Now, I don't recommend that anyone who prays for the sick should arbitrarily punch someone in the stomach. Clearly, that is what God told Brother Copeland to do in that specific situation. The point I want to make is this: we must always wait until our faith is at its highest point before we release it—and we must always release it precisely as God instructs us.

I remember speaking at one of Brother Copeland's Believers Conventions in Fort Worth many years later. I had just preached a message on demonstrating the defeat of Satan, and I was ministering with a particularly strong anointing to people who had formed a long line for prayer. At the opposite end of the line from where I stood was an individual who was being disruptive. I heard and saw the perverted things he was saying and doing. I recognized it was a devil trying to draw attention to itself, to get the people to move their focus away from faith and believing God for their miracle.

My initial thought was to go directly to the other end of the line and do something about it, but instead I listened to what the Lord had to say. "Don't do anything," He told me. "Just tell the people, 'Don't let that devil distract you; we'll deal with it.'" That's what I did, and then I kept on praying.

All the while, this individual was still acting up and causing a commotion. Some of the people were distracted and totally focused on what was happening instead of being focused on God. But I kept praying as that guy just went on and on.

Finally there was a quiet moment, and that's when I heard God say, "Catch him off guard." The next thing I knew, I was standing right in front of the guy, casting the devil out of him. To this day I have no idea how I got there in front of him. One moment I was praying for people at one end of the line, and the next moment I was standing in front of this guy, casting out the devil. Once that devil went out, the man was totally set free. I don't think I would have gotten the same results if I'd laid my hands on him without first hearing what the Spirit of God had to say.

God's instructions are always important, whether you are praying for the sick or casting out devils. When Jesus performed His first miracle of turning water to wine, Mary said to His servants, "Whatever He says to you, do it" (John 2:5). When the Lord says something to me, I've learned to do it—quickly and quietly. No questioning. No debating. No trying to explain to others what I'm doing. I just do it.

I learned to pray for the sick during those early days of working with Kenneth Copeland, and I'm still practicing what I learned way back then.

Tapping into the Wisdom of God

From time to time while I was working with Brother Copeland, he would invite me to go somewhere with him to spend some time in prayer.

In the beginning, I often wondered what he did when he was alone in his hotel room each afternoon praying. That's why spending time with him in prayer was such a great privilege.

Jesus instructed His followers to watch and pray, and that's just what I did with Brother Copeland: I watched him like a hawk. All the time I was watching and listening, I was also learning. Of course, there would be times when he'd say, "Now, Jerry, you pray." Then I would pray. He was teaching me how to pray and how to tap into the wisdom of God.

Through spending time with him in prayer, I learned that any time he came up against something he didn't know how to handle, he spent a lot of time praying in the Holy Ghost, or praying in the Spirit as we often refer to the act of praying in tongues. After one of those times of prayer with Brother Copeland, I made the following note in my journal: "He prays in the Spirit until his mind becomes fruitful."

The apostle Paul said, "For if I pray in a tongue, my spirit prays, but my understanding is unfruitful" (1 Corinthians 14:14). This simply means that while you're praying in the Spirit, in other tongues, your mind has no clue what you are saying. Your mind is unfruitful.

But Paul also says, "For he who speak in a tongue does not speak to men but to God, for no one understands him; however, in the spirit he speaks mysteries" (1 Corinthians 14:2). In other words, when you are praying in the Holy Ghost, you are speaking mysteries. The Amplified Bible says that you are speaking "secret truths and hidden things [not obvious to the understanding]."

Think about this: Colossians 2:3 says that in Christ is hidden the wisdom of God. Where is Christ? He is in you. This means you walk around every day with God's wisdom inside you. Jesus said, "He who believes in Me, as the Scripture has said, out of his heart will flow rivers of living water" (John 7:38). When you are praying in the Holy Ghost, those living waters come forth. They contain the mysteries—the secret truths and hidden things—that will enable you to emerge victorious from any battle you may face.

The problem is, up to that point of praying in the Spirit, your mind is unfruitful because you don't understand what you are saying. This is where a lot of people stop the process, telling themselves, "I don't have a clue what I'm saying, and I'm not supposed to; I'm just praying in my heavenly language." This is not true. You *can* understand what you're praying in the Holy Spirit. If you are willing to pray long enough, your mind *will* become fruitful.

Paul said the one who prays in the Spirit speaks mysteries. Now let's see what he said about wisdom: "But we speak the wisdom of God in a mystery, the hidden wisdom which God ordained before the ages" (1 Corinthians 2:7). Just think, every time you pray in the Holy Ghost, God's wisdom is coming out of you. The wisdom that is hidden in Christ is coming forth, and yet at this point your mind is unfruitful.

So what is the remedy for an unfruitful mind? Paul asked this same question, and then he gave us the answer: "So what shall I do? I will pray with the Spirit, but I will also pray with my understanding" (1 Corinthians 14:15 NIV). Paul is not being double-minded when he says he prays in the Spirit and with understanding. He's making a declaration of faith that says, "I *will* pray in the Spirit, and consequently my understanding will become fruitful."

There have been times I've gone into prayer about a situation that's arisen in the ministry, a situation I don't know how to handle in the natural. I'll begin praying in the Spirit even though I may not catch the meaning or gain any understanding at first. But I don't give up. The next opportunity I have to pray, I pray again in the Holy Ghost.

What I Learned *from the men who imparted into me the most*

I keep doing this until my mind becomes fruitful, until the answer comes to my mind.

I remember years ago we were going through a transition in the ministry. I was holding meetings in large convention centers throughout the country, which meant we had a lot more people working for us then than we do now, including a large road crew that traveled with me. I reached the place where I felt like I'd hit a wall; things were not working for me the way they once had. I was not getting the same results, not even financially, that I'd previously been getting.

I knew it was time to get God's wisdom.

Because it was my custom to go to Granbury, Texas, and rent a small cottage by the lake when I needed to hear from God, I did so on this occasion. Armed with my Bible and a legal pad, I began to pray in the Spirit. I did this until these words popped into my mind: Read the book of Ephesians.

I'd read the book of Ephesians many times. I'd preached out of Ephesians many times. But I sat down and started reading Ephesians again. I got to the place where Paul was talking about the body being fitly joined together, compacting and increasing, when the words *compacting* and *increasing* seemed to jump off the page.

The Lord spoke to me and said, "That's what you need to do in your ministry right now. Compact your ministry, and you will increase your effectiveness." He went on to say, "You are doing things—and you've got people doing things—that I haven't called you to do. These efforts are consuming your resources."

I'm the kind of person who can see a need and will do what I can to meet that need if nothing is already being done about it. Now, as I read again Paul's words in the book of Ephesians, I realized God was showing me why His anointing and finances were not flowing as freely in my ministry as they once had. Although I was directing my resources to meet legitimate needs, God had not specifically led me to do some of the things I was doing. My ministry was suffering because I was doing things I was not called to do, things somebody else should have been doing.

Regardless of where God has called you to serve, you have to be careful not to take on a "savior mentality." You can't save everybody. You can't provide something for everybody who has a need. In my case, I had to realize I couldn't create a job for everyone who moved to my city and said, "God told me I'm supposed to work for you." Bottom line: there's a big difference between a *good* idea and a *God* idea.

So I looked at everything I was doing in the ministry, and I started praying. God confirmed those things He wanted me to do. As for the things He had not called me to do—and they were all good things—I either dissolved those works, or I found someone who *was* called to do the work, and I turned that outreach over to that person.

As soon as the transition was complete, everything changed. With a newly compacted ministry, our effectiveness increased, as did our finances, our peace, and the anointing.

I would never have received God's wisdom had I not taken the time to pray in the Holy Ghost until my mind became fruitful. Tapping into the wisdom of God really is just that simple, yet it does require persistence and perseverance.

Obviously, watching Brother Copeland like a hawk throughout those early years made a tremendous impact on me. I observed how he conducted himself in ministry, and I conduct myself the same way, even to this day. From Brother Copeland, I learned how to preach with authority, how to pray for the sick, and most importantly, how to tap into the wisdom of God by praying in the Holy Ghost.

That is just what I was doing as I was driving to Jacksonville Beach for another meeting two years after my family and I had first driven there from Shreveport at Brother Copeland's invitation. I don't know how long I'd been praying in the Spirit before I heard the Lord ask,

What I Learned from the men who imparted into me the most

"Are you ready?"

"I'm ready," I answered. I knew exactly what He was talking about.

When I got to Jacksonville, I picked up Brother Copeland at the airport and, as I always did, drove him to the hotel and then back to the service again. The next morning before I left my hotel room to take him to the meeting, the phone rang. It was Brother Copeland.

"Are you ready?" he asked.

"Yes, sir," I said.

"Do you know what I'm asking if you're ready for?"

"Yes, sir," I said again. God had already spoken to me on the drive to Jacksonville.

"You're teaching this morning's service."

"Yes, sir, I know that," I said. "God told me that."

Then he said, "I'll go to the service with you. I'll introduce you, and then you'll do the teaching."

I thought, he's going to be in the service while I'm teaching? I'm going to be teaching his sermons! So I said, "Brother Copeland, you don't have to go. I don't need any introduction. I'll just take it."

"No, I want to introduce you to the people. This is your first time to teach, but from now on you will teach the morning services."

The matter was settled.

Brother Copeland went with me to the service and introduced me. For the first five minutes I could barely remember my own name, but then the anointing kicked in. I didn't fully realize it had happened until after the service when he said to me, "You did a masterful job."

I thought, wow—Kenneth Copeland thinks I did a masterful job!

That was the moment that marked the beginning of my teaching ministry.

I will always be grateful to Kenneth Copeland for all the things he taught me. Not only that, but I will never cease to be thankful for how he took me into his life and for teaching me like a son. He continues to be a wonderful example of a true man of God. My love for him, his family, and his ministry is unending.

4

Kenneth E. Hagin

It was through the ministry of Kenneth Copeland that I first learned about Kenneth E. Hagin. In fact, Brother Copeland talked about him so often in his messages that my thought was, if this man has impacted Brother Copeland so much, then I need to listen to him too.

My first encounter with Kenneth Hagin was while we were living in Shreveport. Several days after Terri's fingers had been severed, we received a small post card announcing Kenneth Hagin was going to be speaking in Tyler, Texas.

I didn't know anything about Brother Hagin's ministry other than what I'd heard on Brother Copeland's tapes. I certainly wasn't on his mailing list, so I don't know how that card got addressed to me. But when Carolyn and I read it, we both knew we were supposed to be in that meeting.

Tyler was only ninety-seven miles from Shreveport, less than two hours by car. But the problem was, our car wasn't running. The engine had just blown up, and we had no way to get to Tyler. I prayed, "God, I know you want me in this meeting. What are we supposed to do?"

What I Learned *from the men who imparted into me the most*

I told Carolyn, "We learned from Brother Copeland that faith without works is dead. We're supposed to be at this meeting tonight, so let's get dressed and ready. Then we'll sit in the living room with our Bibles and believe God is going to get us there." And that's just what we did.

As we were sitting on the sofa in our little living room, thanking God for making a way to get us to Tyler, Texas, the phone rang. It was a woman who'd been attending our Monday night Bible studies. She said, "Jerry, I'm about to buy a car from someone, and I want to make sure it's a good one. I heard Kenneth Hagin is going to be speaking tonight at a hotel in Tyler, Texas, and I wondered if you and Carolyn might like to go with me so we can check out the car and hear Kenneth Hagin speak."

I said, "That's God! Come on over."

In less than an hour we were all headed down the interstate to Tyler, Texas, excited that we would soon be seeing Kenneth Hagin for the first time. We were pretty sure the meeting room would be filled, so we started confessing we would have front row seats. I not only like to listen, I like to watch. I wanted to see how Brother Hagin conducted himself, how he preached, how he prayed.

We arrived at the little hotel in downtown Tyler where Brother Hagin was holding his meeting. When we entered the meeting room, which seated about a hundred people, an usher met us and said, "I'm so sorry, but the place is full and we have no more seats." We just looked at each other and grinned.

Almost immediately, another man approached us and said, "I just found three chairs, but the only place to put them is in front of the first row." Carolyn and I knew this was God's way of confirming that we were to be there.

Brother Hagin's message was entitled "How to Write Your Own Ticket with God." He talked about how we can release the God kind of faith by the words we speak. As I sat there that night, watching and listening to Brother Hagin for the first time, I knew this was more than a one-time experience. Somehow, someday, God would make a connection between me and this great man of God.

I listened intently as he preached a message based on Mark 11:23–24: "For assuredly, I say to you, whoever says to this mountain, 'Be removed and be cast into the sea,' and does not doubt in his heart, but believes that those things he says will be done, he will have whatever he says. Therefore I say to you, whatever things you ask when you pray, believe that you receive them, and you will have them."

This is the foundational scripture verse that Brother Hagin's ministry was known for. He preached it so consistently throughout the years of his ministry that he became known affectionately as the father of the twentieth century faith movement.

We learned three specific New Testament truths about faith that night. First, there is the *word of faith,* which is the message. Second is the *law of faith,* which is the application. And finally is the *Spirit of faith,* which is the lifestyle. I believe the Spirit of faith that was on Kenneth Hagin came upon me that night.

What Carolyn and I needed most at that precise time in our lives was to be strengthened in our faith. We were scheduled to take Terri back to the surgeon who had treated her severed fingertips the next day, and we were believing for a miracle of total restoration. Based on Kenneth Copeland's teaching on Mark 11:23–24, we'd put into practice placing a guard over our vocabulary, speaking God's Word over the situation, and believing we could have what we said. But Kenneth Hagin took our understanding of this scripture to a whole new level. He told us how he'd first learned the faith principle of believing you receive *when you pray* and how he'd applied this principle throughout the years. The resulting testimonies he shared lifted our own faith for miracles even higher.

When we left the meeting that night, we were so high in the Spirit and our faith was so energized that we knew we would have our miracle when we took Terri to the doctor. And as I already said in chapter 2, sure enough, when the doctor removed the bandages, her little fingertips were totally restored—complete with tiny little fingernails. The only evidence her fingers had suffered any trauma was in the form of two little scars under the nails.

When I saw those scars, I said, "That's the token of my covenant with God." I knew every time I looked at those scars, I would be reminded that God is not a man that He should lie and that I have a covenant with Almighty God.

I've shared this story many times throughout the years. Whenever Terri has been present, from her childhood to adulthood, I've had her stand up and show her beautiful, fully restored fingers. Recently when Terri was going through airport security on her way to Minneapolis, it was required that she be fingerprinted. I received a text from her saying, "Daddy, the officer said I don't have fingerprints on two of my fingers, and it's the ones that were cut off!"

Even though I didn't get to meet Kenneth Hagin the night I attended his meeting in Tyler, I knew a divine connection had been made in the Spirit. The next time I was in one of his meetings was after our family had moved to Fort Worth and I was working for Brother Copeland. Brother Hagin was scheduled to conduct a series of meetings at Pastor Bob Nichols's church, Calvary Temple, which was located in an old, abandoned post office on the opposite corner from Brother Copeland's office.

We decided our entire family, along with the Copelands, would go to the meeting together. As always, I was believing for a seat on the front row. The church was set up with chairs in front of the podium, which were already filled. But over to the side was a section reserved for overflow, and when they opened it up, we were able to get seats on the front row. I not only got to hear Brother Hagin preach, I got to watch him and observe how he prayed for the sick.

I didn't meet him during those meetings, although Brother Copeland would approach him, shake his hand, and then talk with him. He never introduced me to Kenneth Hagin, but that was all right with me. I knew I would meet him one day, and when it happened, I wanted it to be a God thing, not something I made happen.

I'd read the scripture that said, "A man's gift makes room for him, and brings him before great men" (Proverbs 18:16). I'd say, "God, I don't want Brother Copeland to make this happen, and I'm not going to make it happen. If I'm to meet Kenneth Hagin, it will be because my gift brings me before great men."

I decided, until the time came when I would meet Brother Hagin, I would listen to his messages and observe him anytime I had the opportunity to do so.

Stick with What God Tells You to Do

One of the things I observed about Kenneth Hagin was his willingness and obedience to preach the same message and tell the same stories again and again.

Some people didn't like this; they wanted him to preach about something else besides faith. But not me. I always knew what he was going to preach about, and I couldn't wait to hear what he had to say. In fact, because I knew most of his stories word for word, if he had ever stopped in the middle of a message and asked me to take over, I could have done it without missing a beat.

I'd heard him talk about being born in McKinney, Texas, and being healed in McKinney, Texas, so often that I almost believed I'd been born in McKinney, Texas, too! I never tired of hearing those stories, but what impressed me was he had no inhibitions about preaching the same message and telling the same stories—word for word—over and over. It wasn't until I heard him say, "God raised me up from a deathbed and told me to teach His people faith," that I understood why he did this. He was being obedient to God. His messages and stories were faith building. He was fulfilling the assignment he'd been given by God.

The Bible says, "So then faith come by hearing, an hearing by the word of God" (Romans 10:17). That's what Brother Hagin was doing by preaching the same messages and telling the same stories. He was building our faith. God told him, "Teach my people faith," and each time I heard the message Brother Hagin preached, I always walked away with my faith energized.

He was often asked, "Every time I hear you, you preach on Mark 11:23 and 24. When are you going to preach something else?"

Brother Hagin's response was always the same: "As soon as everyone gets this, we'll move on to something new." He kept preaching Mark 11:23–24 for the next sixty years.

Watching Kenneth Hagin taught me this: stick with what God tells you to do. Don't become distracted with what other people want you to do. Stay with what God wants. As a minister, it's oftentimes easy to be influenced by people. They want you to preach certain things, and there are other things they don't want you to preach. Kenneth Hagin never allowed himself to become distracted by what people wanted him to do. He just stuck with what God wanted him to do.

In 1979 God opened the door for me to meet Brother Hagin. Kenneth Copeland had scheduled a conference in Anaheim, California, and he'd invited both me and Brother Hagin to join him as speakers.

Leave it to God to create a funny situation to put me at ease. As Brother Copeland introduced me to the audience on the first day, he said, "When I first met Jerry, he had about as much anointing as a duck." Everyone laughed, including me, but when I finished preaching and began praying for the people, many were being healed. That's when

Brother Hagin went to the podium and announced, "Well, I tell you one thing: that duck can sure quack now!"

That one statement by Brother Hagin is what first brought us together and marked the beginning of our relationship. And how thankful I have always been to God for arranging that great opportunity.

Although Kenneth E. Hagin went to be with the Lord in 2003, I still listen to his messages today. I have his messages, as well as those of my other mentors and heroes, downloaded on my iPod. I carry those messages in my shirt pocket, and I can listen whenever I want to. Sometimes I'll be sitting on an airplane, listening to Brother Hagin tell one of his stories, and I'll start laughing out loud.

A flight attendant once asked, "What are you laughing at?"

"Bible stories," I told her.

"I didn't know Bible stories were funny."

"They are when this man tells them," I said.

I was laughing again on another flight, and I overheard one flight attendant tell another, "Don't give him anything else to drink, he's already on something." Well, I hadn't had a thing to drink; I was just listening to one of Brother Hagin's messages. And despite the fact that I've heard them probably hundreds of times over the years, I never get tired of listening.

Be Sensitive to the Holy Spirit

From time to time, following one of Brother Hagin's services, Carolyn and I would be invited along with several others back to his hotel room to join him and his wife, Oretha, for a bite to eat.

During these special times of fellowship while Brother Hagin was telling us stories, the Holy Ghost would sometimes come upon him. When this happened, we could actually see him move into the realm of the Spirit. Sometimes we would just sit there quietly and watch; no one uttered a word. There were other times when we sensed his communion with the Spirit was private, and we would all get up and quietly leave the room.

Each time we left the room, I'd think, I wish I knew the Holy Ghost like that; I wish I had that kind of relationship with the Holy Spirit. Then it occurred to me that I could—if I just learned to do what Brother Hagin did. So when the opportunity presented itself, I asked him, "Brother Hagin, it seems like you just get into the Spirit so effortlessly and you fellowship with the Holy Ghost with such ease. How is it that you are so sensitive to Him?"

"Because I pray in the Spirit a lot," he said. "Remember, Paul said, 'I thank my God I speak with tongues more than you all' (Romans 14:18). Pray in the Holy Ghost like Paul did, and you'll become more sensitive to Him."

There were times when a group of us would join Brother Hagin in the speakers' room following a meeting. He would be talking to us, and then he would just start praying in the Spirit as we sat quietly and watched. Sometimes he would prophesy and tell us what the Holy Ghost had said; other times he would say, "Well, boys, you'll hear it tomorrow in the service." His sensitivity to the Holy Spirit made a lasting impression on me and on my ministry.

I'd learned the importance of praying in the Holy Ghost by watching Brother Copeland pray, but now, once again, Brother Hagin was demonstrating another biblical truth at a deeper level. There is just no way to increase our sensitivity to the Holy Spirit without spending deliberate time praying in the Spirit. I learned this first by watching Kenneth Copeland and then by observing Kenneth Hagin.

I will forever be thankful for learning to appreciate this precious gift that God has given us: His Holy Spirit.

Purpose to Walk in Love

I don't know if there's ever been another preacher who has been more persecuted for teaching the word of faith than Kenneth Hagin. I know because I saw it. I was actually in meetings where it happened. I also saw some of the ugly letters that were written to him. I witnessed entire denominations verbally crucify him for preaching the word of faith, and yet I never once heard him lash out at his critics.

He just walked in love.

I know a little about persecution myself, and I can tell you that walking in love is not an easy thing to do. When it seems everyone is criticizing and persecuting you for your faith, it's not easy to refrain from retaliating. Your flesh wants nothing more than to say something ugly about them or to preach about them in your next service. But Kenneth Hagin never would. He just purposed to walk in love, and he refused to get into strife.

The more people criticized his message of faith, the more he preached it. He just kept preaching his message no matter what people said to him or about him—or what they wrote. He never changed his message to satisfy the critics or to win favor with those who fought him the hardest.

The closest thing to retaliation I ever heard Brother Hagin say was, "Well, bless their poor hearts and their stupid heads. They just don't know any better." He spoke even those words with gentle humor, never specifically directing his comments to any particular person. That was about as harsh as he ever was.

A lot of his critics came and went. A lot of them made a big splash and then fizzled out. But Brother Hagin purposed to walk in love, and he kept right on walking in love and preaching the word of faith until the day he went home to be with Jesus. I'm so thankful that he did.

See the Potential in God's Young Ministers

I remember going to Tulsa in the late 1970s, shortly after Buddy and Pat Harrison founded a church they named Faith Christian Fellowship.

What I Learned *from the men who imparted into me the most*

Carolyn and I had become friends with Buddy and his wife, Pat, who was brother Hagin's daughter. I was pleased when they invited me to come and preach for three nights at their church.

Faith Christian Fellowship had become a model "Word of Faith" church, a term that was becoming widely recognized and rapidly growing in popularity. When I walked out on the platform that first night, there were Brother Hagin and his wife, Oretha, sitting on the front row of the auditorium. I was surprised to learn they would be in my service, and even more surprised when they returned for the other two services.

At the conclusion of the final night's service, I walked up to Brother Hagin and said, "I'm so honored that you would come to hear me."

I'll never forget what he said: "Oh, I always get something out of your preaching."

I thought, Kenneth Hagin gets something out of my preaching?

Oretha said, "He really likes you, he does. He gets a lot out of your preaching."

Talk about making a person feel good. Here's one of my mentors—I've learned much of what I know through his books and tapes—and now he tells me he always gets something out of my preaching.

Not too long afterward, in 1981, he walked up to me and said, "You're one of those in the Word of Faith who is going to make a big impact. I'm inviting you to come and speak in my next campmeeting, and it will be for you like a shot of penicillin."

I knew exactly what Brother Hagin meant. In other words, he was going to introduce my ministry to an audience that had never heard of me. That introduction would expose my gift to those whom he felt needed to hear what I had to say. I was both humbled and honored by the mere thought that Kenneth Hagin believed in me. Later he asked me to preach in another campmeeting and also in some of his "mini-faith seminars," which he conducted all over the country.

It was Brother Hagin who taught me the value of seeing potential in God's young ministers. One of my most vivid memories was sitting with an esteemed group of seasoned ministers who were together in a room where Brother Hagin was doing most of the talking. As a young minister, I'd gone into that meeting determined I wasn't going to say a thing; I was just going to listen and learn.

When we took a break for lunch, Brother Hagin slipped his arm around me and said, "Now, Brother Jerry, you're just talking too much; you need to let others have the floor." Of course, he was kidding me, because I hadn't said a word.

"Brother Hagin," I answered, "if I have something to say, I'll say it."

He smiled and said, "I knew you were that way."

When we got back to the meeting, he said, "We haven't heard from Brother Jerry today. Brother Jerry, what do you think?"

I would have left that meeting without saying a word, but Brother Hagin saw potential in me. He encouraged me.

If you are a young minister, let me encourage you to glean all that you can from those who have been used by God for a long time. Be a good listener and be a doer of what you learn. God will honor your faith and your obedience just as He has honored theirs.

Increase by Association

Anyone who has ever heard Kenneth Hagin preach will tell you that just being around the man would cause your faith to go to another level, and I found this to be true for me.

I've learned that faith is contagious. The Bible says, "He that walketh with wise men shall be wise" (Proverbs 13:20). This is why I so cherished every opportunity I had to spend time with the man known as the father of the twentieth century faith movement. It is why I believe in what I call the law of increase by association.

Over the course of time, Carolyn and I developed a warm and close relationship with Kenneth and Oretha Hagin. Anytime we were with the Hagins, we always gleaned something from them. I remember one particular time during the early days of our relationship when we were privileged to have them in our home with a small group of other ministers. Our girls were young and had to go to school the next day. When Carolyn told them it was time to go to bed, they went to their room, put on their pajamas and robes, and then came back and pleaded to stay up and listen to Brother Hagin tell his stories.

I'll never forget the sight. Brother Hagin was leaning back in the recliner in our den, with Oretha at his side. Buddy and Pat Harrison were there, along with Happy and Jeanne Caldwell and Norvel Hayes. And there were both of my little daughters, on the floor in front of Brother Hagin. They were lying on their stomachs with their chins propped on their hands, holding to his every word until three o'clock in the morning. All of us who had gathered there that evening, both young and old, were increased in faith by our association with Brother Hagin.

Another time I was taking part in a meeting of ministers that included Kenneth Copeland, Kenneth Hagin, T.L. Osborn, John Osteen, Fred Price, and several other well-known individuals. Also in the room with us were six young ministers. None of these young men were seasoned in ministry, yet we could all clearly see in them the potential to impact lives for the Lord.

As the meeting proceeded, I noticed it was these younger ministers who were doing most of the talking. I thought, here we have a room full of spiritual giants, and these young men are doing more talking than listening.

Finally, someone said, "Brother Hagin, don't you have anything to say?"

"Well, I wasn't sure if you wanted to hear me, but, yes, I do," he replied.

Brother Hagin said more in the next five minutes than the others had said in the previous two hours combined. I learned a valuable lesson at that meeting: when you are around great men, listen to them; don't talk unless you are called on. What could I have possibly told Kenneth Hagin about faith that he didn't already know?

The last opportunity I had to be in one of Kenneth Hagin's meetings before he went home to be with the Lord was in Miami, Florida, at Pastor Stan Moore's church. I was sitting on the front row in an aisle seat when Brother Hagin stepped down from the platform and continued preaching as he walked back and forth across the front of the auditorium. Then he stopped in the aisle and put his hand on my shoulder. For the next fifteen minutes he stood there like that, leaning on me while he was teaching. He would walk away and preach a little bit, and then he'd return to my side, place his hand upon me, and teach for another fifteen minutes.

After the service, his daughter, Pat, said, "You know why he does that, don't you?"

"Why?" I asked.

"Because he feels comfortable with you. He likes you. Every time you come to one of his services, I see him drawn to you."

I thought, wow—what an honor. Kenneth Hagin is comfortable with me.

One time Oretha told me the reason he was comfortable with me was that I don't talk much. She said, "You know, Brother Hagin doesn't talk much. He just twiddles his thumbs while everyone else is talking, and he doesn't speak until he has something to say. That's the reason he likes you; you're a good listener, and you don't talk much."

Even though Brother Hagin is in heaven today, I still listen to his teachings on Mark 11:23 and 24. My faith is still energized when I listen to him. And it is my privilege to share the things I learned while being in his meetings and preaching with him. I learned some things by observation, and other things I learned from reading and listening to his materials.

You can learn so much by reading books and listening to other people's resources. Just don't ever get to the place where you think you know all you need to know. One of the things I appreciated about Brother Hagin was his willingness to keep learning. I remember when he said to me, "I always get something out of your teaching." I knew right then and there that although this man had probably forgotten more about faith than I had yet learned, he was still learning, and he valued the knowledge he could glean from others.

Shortly after Brother Hagin went home to be with the Lord, I asked my adult daughters, Jerriann and Terri, both of whom are in the ministry today, "What was your most memorable time with Brother Hagin?"

Without hesitation, they said, "In our den, lying on our stomachs, listening to Brother Hagin tell faith stories until three in the morning."

Kenneth Hagin was indeed a father of faith to our generations.

5

Oral Roberts

Of the many wonderful people I've known throughout my life, Oral Roberts is one of my favorites. I consider him my spiritual grandfather, because he first taught Kenneth Copeland, who in turn taught me, many of the principles upon which my ministry has been founded. It was such a joy and honor for Carolyn and me to know this outstanding man of God and his darling wife, Evelyn. What a great team they were.

I saved every letter Oral Roberts wrote to me over the years, all handwritten. Each one of them was signed, "Your partner, Oral Roberts." He and Evelyn generously supported our ministry until they went to be with the Lord.

I find it amazing when I think about the impact this man made on my life. What are the odds of a ten-year-old boy standing in his grandmother's home in Oklahoma City on Thanksgiving Day, watching for the first time as this great man preached on TV, hearing the call of God, and then years later, having Oral Roberts become his partner? That's just God!

In 1969, immediately after surrendering my life to the Lord and beginning my walk of faith for full-time ministry, I started watching Oral Roberts on TV. I'd not actually watched him since that encounter I had with God in 1957, but because it was through his ministry that I heard the call of God saying I would someday preach and pray like Oral Roberts, I decided I needed to start following his ministry and listening to his teaching.

I remember watching Brother Roberts's program one day when he was introducing his new book, *The Miracle of Seed Faith*. At the end of the broadcast he said, "If you'll write and ask me for a copy, I'll send it to you absolutely free."

I looked at Carolyn and said, "There's one we can afford." So she wrote to Oral Roberts Evangelistic Association, and sure enough, they sent us a copy of the book.

That little book turned out to be life-changing for us. Through it we learned how to make God our total source of supply. Brother Roberts taught that faith was like a seed and there was great value in sowing seed. Using Jesus' words "if you have faith as a mustard seed" (Luke 17:6), Brother Roberts taught how faith works.

Up until that time, although I knew Jesus was a great teacher, I just wasn't connecting to His words in my King James Bible. However, when Oral Roberts taught in his own personal style, everything began to make sense to me. He introduced what he called the law of seedtime and harvest, established in the book of Genesis: "While the earth remains, seedtime and harvest . . . shall not cease" (Genesis 8:22).

For me, the law of seedtime and harvest caused Luke 6:38 ("Give, and it will be given to you") to take on a whole new meaning. In fact, after reading *The Miracle of Seed Faith*, I believed I could actually apply this law to sow my way out of debt.

We were in quite a lot of debt in those days. My business had a lot of debts, and Carolyn and I had a lot of personal debts. The amount may not sound like much today, but in 1969, $30,000 was a lot of money. That amount then was like $300,000 today, and in the natural we had no idea how we could ever pay it back—especially since I'd shut down my business and was studying the Bible eight hours a day. Brother Roberts's book was such a blessing to Carolyn and me. Even though we didn't have a whole lot to sow, we made the decision that every time we had the opportunity, we would sow *something*.

We also made the decision to become tithers. Carolyn's parents were faithful tithers and givers who were disciplined in their finances. It was apparent to me how tithing had blessed their lives. As a result of their obedience to God's Word, God did what He said He would do: He opened the windows of heaven and blessed them (see Malachi 3:10).

Carolyn's dad, Olen Creech, was a homebuilder, and I remember the time when things slowed down and he didn't have many jobs. Olen didn't know Oral Roberts, but after hosting Kenneth Copeland in his home, he knew Brother Copeland well enough to call him and say, "I need you to stand in agreement with me, because I need more jobs."

Brother Copeland said, "The next time we're together, I want you to bring your Bible and your checkbook."

"Why do you want me to bring my checkbook?"

"Because we're going to show God all the check stubs from your tithing and giving. We're going to hold those up with the Bible and ask God to honor His Word on your behalf."

So that's just what they did. They sat down together on the living room floor with the Bible and Olen's check stubs. Brother Copeland said, "Jesus, this man is a tither, and Your Word says You'll open the windows of heaven for him and pour out blessing that there will be no room to contain."

A few weeks later, Olen called Brother Copeland and said, "I have so much work that I'm having to refer people to other builders. I can't get to all the work I've got!"

That experience really made an impression on me. Although

What I Learned *from the men who imparted into me the most*

Carolyn knew the principles of debt-free living, I was just starting out in my faith walk. I knew it might not be easy at first, but I was determined to apply the law of seedtime and harvest I'd learned from Oral Roberts to get out of debt.

Until that time, the only way I knew to exist was by borrowing money. My dad had taken me to the bank to get my first loan when I was eighteen years old. I needed the money to start my first semester of college, and I put up my 1957 Chevy as collateral.

When Carolyn and I first married, I didn't realize I was making wrong decisions when I continued to borrow for everything we needed. Living debt free was just not the way I was brought up; it was not the way my parents lived. But now, this new concept—the miracle of seed faith—showed me a way to get out of debt by sowing my way into abundance. Getting into abundance became my quest.

I couldn't get enough of Brother Roberts's teaching on the law of seedtime and harvest. As Carolyn and I put it to practice, we began to see results. We didn't get out of debt overnight. We didn't get out of debt in a month or even six months. But as we were obedient to tithe and sow seed at God's direction, God continued to manifest His blessing. I'll never forget the day I walked into the bank and paid off the last debt from my business. Then, over a period of time, Carolyn and I personally became debt free.

The seed-faith lifestyle began working for us the moment we applied the law of seedtime and harvest, and we've continued to live that lifestyle for forty-five years. It is wonderful to be debt free. It's wonderful to have a ministry that is debt free. Hardly a day goes by that this ministry is not sowing seed into somebody else's life or ministry. I thank God for Oral Roberts and his obedience to boldly proclaim God's Word and to teach the law of seedtime and harvest.

My admiration for Oral Roberts began during those early days when I was beginning my walk with the Lord. I highly respected him, but I never dreamed I would ever meet the man. After all, he was Oral Roberts. At that time, Oral Roberts and Billy Graham were the two biggest names in Christian ministry. Who meets Billy Graham? Who meets Oral Roberts? I thought it would be wonderful if someday I could just walk up to this man, shake his hand, and say, "Thank you, sir. I'm in the ministry because of you."

But God had much more in mind.

Meeting My Mentor

In 1981, I was preaching with Kenneth Copeland in Charlotte, North Carolina, at his East Coast Believers Convention. It was Saturday night, and Brother Copeland was about to close out the last service of the convention, as he always did. But this particular night, when he got up to preach, he just stopped and said, "Jerry, come up here. God wants you to close out the convention."

I had already preached all the messages I'd prepared for that convention, and I didn't have a clue what I was going to preach. But I knew better than to disobey the prophet. So I got up, and as I was walking to the platform, Brother Copeland asked for his assistant to place a chair on the platform, about three feet from the podium. When the chair was in place, Brother Copeland sat on it.

When I got to the podium, I still didn't know what I was going to say, but as I laid down my Bible, it fell open to the book of Daniel. The section heading said, "Three Hebrew Children in the Fiery Furnace." The moment I saw those words, I started preaching the sermon I'd heard Oral Roberts preach that day back in 1957 when I was ten years old, when God first called me to preach. That sermon was in me, and I didn't know it.

I started preaching Oral Roberts's sermon "The Fourth Man," which showed Jesus in every book of the Bible. I even sounded like Oral Roberts. I said, "Who is this fourth man? I'll tell you who He is. In Genesis He is . . . ," and I went through every book of the Bible until I got to the final book. I declared, "In the book of Revelation, He is the King of Kings, the soon coming redeemer, and the Son of the living God!"

That's when the anointing of God hit that place. People started getting out of wheelchairs, just like I'd seen them do in 1957 when I watched Oral Roberts preach the same televised message at a tent crusade. What happened was amazing, and I stood in awe at what had just taken place in my life.

Brother Copeland spoke to his television producer that night and said, "I don't know what you have planned for our *Believers Voice of Victory* program, but cancel it and air the message Jerry just preached as quickly as you can."

Well, in a few weeks my sermon, which was originally Brother Roberts's sermon entitled "The Fourth Man," aired nationwide on a Sunday morning.

First thing Monday morning I got a call from Oral Roberts's secretary saying he wanted to see me in his office that afternoon.

I'd never met the man, so was thinking, they're going to sue me for preaching his message! But I flew to Tulsa and went to his office, where I was greeted by Ruth Rooks, the only secretary he'd ever had. She used the intercom to let him know I was there, and then looked at me and said, "He'll be coming through those doors over there."

I turned in the direction she pointed and saw an impressive set of double doors that looked to be about twelve feet high. A moment later the doors opened, and there stood Oral Roberts, his arms stretched wide.

I knew he was a tall man, but from my perspective, he looked like he was also about twelve feet tall. His outstretched arms seemed to fill the room from one end to the other. I was speechless in his presence, but I'll never forget the first words he spoke to me: "Come, my brother.

I've been wanting to meet you for a long time."

I actually turned around to see who had come into the room behind me, but no one was there but Ruth. And me. And Oral Roberts.

I looked at him and asked, "Me?"

"Yes. I've been wanting to meet you for a long time," he said again.

I thought, you don't even know me. But I walked hesitantly up to him, and he just reached out and grabbed me. He pulled me to his chest and started prophesying over me. When he finished, he released me and ordered, "Follow me into my office."

I thought, this is where he introduces his attorneys and then tells me I'm getting sued for preaching his sermon. But when I stepped into his office, I looked around, and nobody else was there.

"Have a seat," he said.

So I sat on the sofa and then he sat down next to me.

"Yesterday Evelyn and I were watching Kenneth Copeland's broadcast and we saw you preaching my sermon on The Fourth Man."

Dear Lord, here it comes, I thought.

"I turned to Evelyn and said, 'I've never seen anybody preach that sermon better—except me. I've heard about Jerry Savelle. I was told he heard the call of God as a young boy while he was watching me preach. It's time for us to meet this young man.'"

He paused a moment as I sat speechless, trying to take in what he was telling me.

"So that's why I called," he continued. "I wanted to meet you and tell you how proud I was watching you preach my sermon, because you reminded me of when I was a young man, preaching under the big tent."

So he hadn't called me to Tulsa to tell me he was going to sue me? I couldn't help but cry. Here's the man I'd watched on my grandmother's TV when I heard God's call at the age of ten, and now he's sitting next to me, telling me he believes in me.

Only God can do things like that.

The Three Keys to Success

Throughout the years I had the honor to preach occasionally with Oral Roberts, and on one of those occasions my message was "The Three Keys to Success." After I finished preaching, Brother Roberts asked, "Where did you get those three keys?"

"From Kenneth Copeland," I proudly announced.

I went on to tell him about the first time I'd heard them. I was driving Brother Copeland from a meeting back to our hotel when he reached over and hit me on my shoulder. At first I thought I was driving the wrong way or doing something wrong. Brother Copeland looked at me with those piercing eyes and said, "I'm going to give you the three keys to success."

I was driving the car and had no way to write down what he was about to say, so I told myself I had the mind of Christ and I'd remember every word he said (which I did).

"Number one," Brother Copeland said. "Find out the will of God. Number two: once you know God's will, confer no more with flesh and blood. And number three: get the job done at any cost."

Then he turned around and didn't say another word. He didn't expound; that was it.

Brother Roberts listened to my account patiently, and then with a smile he said, "Well, he got those three keys from me."

I just shook my head and smiled right back at him, amazed at the legacy of faith that had passed from Brother Roberts to Brother Copeland and then to me. For decades I've had the opportunity to apply those three keys consistently in both my personal life and my ministry, and I can attest to their veracity.

Finding the will of God is the foundation on which every endeavor must be built. I'm often asked, "Brother Jerry, how do you find the will of God?" There are several avenues I use when I'm seeking the will of God, beginning with praying in the Holy Ghost. This is something that believers can never do too much. As I've already said, I pray in the Spirit until my mind becomes fruitful.

After praying in the Spirit, I always turn to God's Word to see if there is a situation in the Bible similar to the one I'm dealing with. The Holy Spirit may lead me to a passage where God gives specific instructions about how to deal with a matter. Or He may bring to my remembrance someone I know personally who has gone through the same situation. If what He told them to do bears witness with my spirit, that is what I also do.

Brother Hagin used to talk about this inward witness. I learned a long time ago that God is not the author of confusion; He is the author of peace. In anything I do, I always follow the direction that produces the inner witness of peace. If there is confusion, I don't move. Where there is confusion, there is fear. Fear activates Satan, just like faith activates God. If I don't have peace about going a certain direction, then I don't go. I'd like to say I'm 100 percent accurate every time, but that's not the case. Sometimes I go through a process of elimination, which is ultimately determined by the direction that produces the greatest peace.

When the will of God has been established and confirmed by that inner witness of peace, there is no need to confer with flesh and blood. Brother Roberts got this revelation in the book of Galatians, where Paul said, "But when it pleased God . . . to reveal His Son in me, that I might preach Him among the Gentiles, I did *not immediately confer with flesh and blood*, nor did I go up to Jerusalem to those who were apostles before me" (Galatians 1:15–17 italics added).

To "not confer with flesh and blood" simply means you are not to open yourself up to negative suggestions from other people. Once you have established the will of God in your situation, it's best to keep it to yourself for a while. Not everyone is going to be as enthusiastic about it as you are. Not everyone will agree you've heard from God.

What I Learned from the men who imparted into me the most

Once you announce your plans and ask others what they think—particularly if they are not on the same spiritual level with you—you could open yourself to distraction and discouragement. Worse than that, you could be talked out of what God has instructed you to do.

There are, however, times when it is wise to go to someone you know is on a higher spiritual level than you are, and ask the person to pray over the matter. For instance, I've gone to Brother Copeland and said, "Here is what I'm sensing the Lord wants me to do. I'd appreciate it if you would pray over it, and if you pick up anything from the Lord, let me know."

I'm certainly not going to go to someone who's not yet sure if they really do believe God. I'm not going to share what God has told me with someone who is going to try to talk me out of it. As Brother Roberts said, "I will confer no more with flesh and blood."

Finally, we are to get the job done at any cost. This means no compromise. Whatever it takes. Regardless of how long it takes. If we have to persevere for days, weeks, months, or years, quitting is never an option. Not when we have a God who is faithful to His Word and to His promises.

These three keys to success originated with Oral Roberts, who taught them to Kenneth Copeland, who taught them to me. Brother Copeland still practices these keys, and so do I. I've taught them to ministers all over the world who have sent many marvelous testimonies of how they practice these keys themselves and teach them as Brother Roberts did, without compromise, to a new generation of believers.

A Noncompromising Stand

I often heard Oral Roberts say, "If you won't bow, then you won't burn." This saying came from his message "The Fourth Man" and referred to the three Hebrew children who refused to bow to another god. This was Brother Roberts's way of saying, "Don't ever compromise."

One of the greatest truths he taught me was this: what you compromise to obtain, you will ultimately lose. In other words, if you give in to the pressure to make something happen for yourself, you usually wind up losing it. He was adamant about not compromising, and he loved to give what he called an "Oral exam" to see if someone was really listening, comprehending, and retaining what he was teaching.

For instance, I was once seated next to him on a flight to London when he finished a book he'd been reading. He turned to me and said, "Jerry, I want you to read this before we get to London, and when we get there, I'll ask you questions." I remember confessing to myself that I had the mind of Christ and I would remember every word. So I read the book and then I took the "Oral exam." Thank God, I answered all of his questions correctly.

Brother Roberts was also known for giving an "Oral exam" after he preached. If someone walked up to him and said, "That was a great message, sir," he would immediately reply with "What were my three main points and the three scriptures that went with them?" Of course, most people couldn't answer.

I remember one time when I set up my friend, Jesse Duplantis. I invited him and his wife, Cathy, to our home to share a meal with Brother Roberts after he'd preached one of his messages. As expected, Jesse said, "That was a great sermon." And as I knew he would, Brother Roberts asked Jesse to name his three main points and the supporting scriptures. I sat there laughing, but Jesse actually did pretty well. His answers satisfied Brother Roberts

Not only would Oral Roberts test to see if someone was listening to him, he'd also test to see whether or not a person was willing to compromise. One time we were about to enter a board of regents meeting at Oral Roberts University when Brother Roberts pulled me aside and asked me to make a particular statement in the meeting. I knew the information he gave me was not accurate, so I said, "Brother

Roberts, I can't do that." I didn't realize at the time he was just testing me.

"Why not?" he asked.

"Because it's not entirely true," I told him.

"But I told you to say it."

"I know you did. I'm not trying to dishonor you, but what you want me to say is not entirely accurate, and I'm not going to say it."

I couldn't believe what happened next. He turned his head away and refused to look at me. Then he walked away from me. And I *really* couldn't believe what I did next, but I grabbed him and turned him around and said, "I'm not saying that. If you call on me, I'm not going to say it!"

Then he just grinned and said, "That's what I love about you. You won't compromise."

I said, "You were just testing me to see if I would give in."

"I knew you wouldn't," he said.

Brother Roberts also had a way of catching a person off guard and stretching that person at the same time. In my case, he wanted to see if I would bow to the pressure of "Oral Roberts said do it," and I didn't. I loved being around him because he always stretched me to be better and yet never compromise.

There were times in my ministry when I was going through something—maybe a financial challenge—and there seemed no way in the natural to overcome it. I would get on a plane and fly to Tulsa, where I'd get an upper-level room in the hotel right across the street from the ORU campus. And then I'd sit there in a chair and just look at the sprawling 263-acre campus with its 60-foot tall praying hands sculpture and the soaring City of Faith central tower.

I'd put a second chair next to mine; it was for the devil. And I'd say to him, "Now, you've been telling me when I'm at home how faith can't do what God has told me to do. Just look across the street and see what faith did. Look at that campus. Faith built that."

Of course, the devil didn't want to hear or see any of this. That's when I'd say, "Where are you going? You started this. Don't leave yet!"

I'd go to Tulsa and would never even talk to Oral Roberts. My own faith and resolve not to compromise were strengthened as I'd sit there looking at what Oral Roberts's faith and his commitment to not compromise had accomplished. Today people come to our facilities in Crowley, Texas, and they can see what faith has done, what God has done.

Never, ever let people of lesser faith pull you down and cause you to compromise. Make a point to get around those who know more than you do, who operate at a greater level of faith than you do, and let them stretch you. You may not have the opportunity to know someone like Oral Roberts personally, but there are plenty of people who can mentor you through their books, CDs, and teaching materials. Don't ever be afraid of being stretched or challenged to go to another level.

That's just what Oral Roberts did every time I was around him.

Think Big

I remember the plaque Brother Roberts kept on his desk that said, "No little plans made here." It was a fitting phrase for a man who was known as a big thinker.

One of the things I learned by observing him was, if he was in the presence of others who were sharing ideas that he viewed as small thinking, he would either turn his head and ignore them, or he would just walk away. Anyone who was going to talk to Oral Roberts had to think big and talk big.

When he was preparing to build the City of Faith Medical and Research Center on the campus of Oral Roberts University, his vision was for a 77-story building with a projected cost of hundreds of millions of dollars. But what's more, Brother Roberts intended to pay cash as he went.

I was on the board at that time and was privileged to watch the process begin. Dr. James Winslow was the chief physician and the man appointed by Brother Roberts to get everything done. It was not uncommon for the Lord to show Brother Roberts something in a dream that He wanted for the facility. Brother Roberts would describe what he'd seen to Dr. Winslow, and it was his responsibility to get it for the hospital. There were numerous times when he would go to a big company, describe a particular piece of equipment and say, "My superior, Oral Roberts, wants this."

The answer was often, "This doesn't exist. You want something that is impossible."

"No," Dr. Winslow would say. "My boss wants the impossible; all I'm asking for is the highly improbable."

Over and over again, God did the impossible. And over and over again, Oral Roberts was criticized. But that criticism was always like water on a duck's back; he just moved forward anyway.

"Why don't they ever talk ugly about you?" he once asked me. "I'm the most hated preacher in America, and all I've ever tried to do was bring healing to my generation. Why don't they blast you like they do me?"

"Brother Roberts, I'm different. I do things quickly and quietly," I told him.

That's when I saw him smile real big. He'd done it again; he was testing me.

"I thrive on criticism," he said. "When they are talking about me the ugliest, that's when I rise to the top."

Oral Roberts was a big thinker, and he expected those around him to be big thinkers too. When I told him of my plans to build a medical facility in Kenya, Brother Roberts said he believed God wanted him to equip it and then staff it with doctors and nurses coming out of ORU. He asked if he could go with me to Kenya, and I said yes. We assembled

Oral Roberts

a team of people and went to Kenya to meet with the president so that we could present our vision and ask him for land to build on.

When we got to the appointed meeting, we were disappointed to learn the president had been called away for an emergency. But the vice president and some of the cabinet members were there to meet with us.

We were all gathered in a room, and I was fully prepared to make my presentation, complete with all the plans for the facility. I couldn't think of anyone I'd want to be with me more than Oral Roberts, the man whose faith had built one of America's most prestigious universities and medical facilities. This was going to be an historic meeting for Jerry Savelle Ministries International.

To justify our need for land, I carefully outlined the plans for an outpatient clinic that could treat two to four hundred patients each day. I could tell I had the full attention of the vice president and the members of the cabinet. The time was right to close the deal, so I boldly asked that the government give us a specific amount of land. That's when I noticed Brother Roberts turn his head like he always did when he thought people were talking too small. But I continued.

In a little while, Brother Roberts grabbed a napkin, wrote something on it, and threw it down at the end of the table. He picked up another napkin, wrote something on it, and again threw it down at the end of the table. He repeated this process yet again—while the vice president of Kenya was speaking—and all I could think was, this is really rude! Here I am, trying to conduct business, and Oral Roberts is either turning his head away or tossing napkins at the end of the table.

Finally, right in the middle of the vice president's discourse, Brother Roberts hit me on the arm, put a napkin in front of me, and said, "Do you know what that says?"

"Brother Roberts, can this wait? The vice president is speaking to us," I said.

"No! Do you know what that says?"

I looked at a line of about a dozen meaningless letters he'd printed on the napkin and said, "I don't have a clue what it says." I pushed the napkin back toward him, thinking, one of us needs to be listening here.

He hit me again and said, "Look at it closely, and tell me what it says."

"Brother Roberts, can this wait until after we are through here?"

He just looked at me and said, "Look at it closely."

I looked at the napkin on which he'd printed the following letters: s-t-r-e-b-o-r-l-a-r-o. Exasperated, I said, "Excuse me, sir, I don't have a clue what those letters say. What do they spell?"

"They spell Oral Roberts backwards," he told me without blinking an eye.

I couldn't believe what I was hearing. "You've been spending all this time spelling your name backwards? Are we boring you?"

"Yes, *you* are boring me. *He* is boring me. Everybody in this room is boring me, because you are all small thinkers!"

I was stunned, but he wasn't finished.

"We can't do this with the amount of land you're asking for," Brother Roberts said. I thought, what do you mean, we? This is *my* project. Then he said, "Tell the man you want ten times the amount of property."

"Well, Brother Roberts, I feel led of the Lord for *you* to tell him we want ten times the amount of property than what I just asked for."

Brother Roberts looked at the vice president and cabinet members and said, "We want ten times the amount of property."

And just like that, they agreed to give it to us.

Jesus said, "Ye have not because ye ask not" (James 4:2 KJV). Since that day in Kenya, anytime people around me are exhibiting their small thinking through their small talking, I just pull out a pen and write e-l-l-e-v-a-s-y-r-r-e-j on a napkin. That's Jerry Savelle spelled backwards.

We serve a big God.

A Servant's Heart

Those who only saw Oral Roberts on television knew him as a great, bold, and authoritative man—which he was. But being with him on various occasions when he would actually do something to serve me, I was privileged to see his servant's heart. I considered myself his subordinate, but he considered me his equal.

He once told me about what his mother used to say as he was becoming widely recognized for his healing ministry: "Oral, always stay small in your own eyes." And from what I saw, he'd followed his mother's advice throughout his entire life.

When we were on that trip to Kenya, I had other things to attend to besides our meeting with the government. I was also conducting a pastors' seminar, dedicating churches we'd built, and breaking ground for churches we were about to build. I told Brother Roberts beforehand, "When we get there, it's not likely I'm going to spend much time with you, but I'll assign someone to stay with you at the hotel."

He said, "That's fine. But if there's anything you want me to do, you just command me to do it."

"Brother Roberts, that's not going to happen. I don't mind you commanding me to do things, but I will never command you to do something."

He looked me right in the eye and said, "Whose trip is this?"

I knew this wasn't a trick question, so I confidently answered, "It's mine."

"Did you invite me to come, or did I invite myself?"

"You invited yourself," I said.

"Then you're in control. This is your mission. This is your trip. This is your meeting, and I'm here to serve you. Whatever you want me to do, command me to do it."

"That's not likely to happen, sir, but thank you."

I proceeded with the pastors' conference as planned, but after three days I realized something: most of the pastors I was ministering to had heard the call of God in 1969 when Oral Roberts had last preached there. I thought, here are all these young Kenyan nationals who are in the ministry because of Oral Roberts, and I've got him sitting at the hotel doing nothing. That's when I decided to have him come to the meeting and lay his hands on them.

When I returned to the hotel, I went to Brother Roberts's room and knocked on the door. When he answered, I said, "I feel a command coming on."

"What do you want me to do?"

"I command you to come and minister to a group of pastors who answered the call to ministry when you were here in 1969. I want you to lay your hands on them and pray for them."

On the way to the meeting, he said, "Now, Jerry, I'm seventy years old. I'm not as young as you are, so I can't preach as long as you do, and I can't lay hands on people as long as you can. But I'll preach and pray as long as I can, though I may have to sit on a stool to do it."

"That's fine," I told him. "You just give them all you can."

When I introduced Brother Roberts to the group, the place went wild. They hadn't known he was even in Kenya. Before he stepped behind the podium, he told me he would preach only about fifteen minutes and then pray for half an hour or so.

An hour and a half later he was still preaching. I walked up to the podium and said, "I command you to stop now and go lay your hands on them." And that's just what he did.

Jesus said, "He who is greatest among you shall be your servant"

(Matthew 23:11). Although Oral Roberts was recognized and reverenced in nations throughout the world, he never lost his servant's heart. I saw this again and again. When Kenneth Copeland and I were together with him, we were like kids, always wanting to do something for him. But he would turn the situation around and do something for us. The last thing we'd expect was that Oral Roberts would carry one of our coats or Bibles to the car for us, but he had a servant's heart. And that's what made him a great man.

Brother Roberts often described himself as a servant of God whose assignment was to take healing to his generation. He expected anyone who was associated with him in any way to know that Jesus was, and still is, a healing Jesus. He also expected those who learned from him to take healing to their generation.

That's why, wherever I go to share the Word of God, I always let others know that Jesus is still a healing Jesus.

6

T.L. Osborn

When Carolyn surrendered her life to the Lord as a little girl, she made a vow to God that the man she would one day marry was going to be born again and filled with the Holy Ghost, preach the gospel, and go to Africa. After I surrendered my life to the Lord in 1969, I wasn't against the idea of going to Africa; I just didn't want to go only because Carolyn wanted me to go. I wanted to know for sure that God wanted me to go.

Shortly after I left Brother Copeland's organization and launched into my own ministry, I was invited to Hot Springs, Arkansas, to preach at an outdoor pavilion on a ranch. I was staying at the home of an elderly couple, the Johnsons, and I asked if there was a place I could go to pray every day.

Mr. Johnson said, "There's a spot at the back of our property where you'll find a small pond and big oak tree. That's where I sometimes go to pray."

"That sounds good to me," I said.

But then Mrs. Johnson said to her husband, "Oh, sweetheart, the grass hasn't been mowed in a long time, and it's so tall now. I don't know if Brother Jerry can even get back there."

"That's all right," I said. "I'll just find a quiet place somewhere to pray tomorrow."

Well, the next morning I was awakened by the sound of a tractor, and when I looked out the window, I saw Mr. Johnson out there brush hogging a path to the pond. He came back a little later and said he had the place ready for me.

Each morning I would walk to the little pond and sit under the oak tree to pray and study in preparation for the evening service. One morning the Lord dropped the idea of missions into my heart, and in particular, the continent of Africa. He said, "There will be ten major African nations you will be involved in, and the springboard is Kenya. That is where you will begin."

When I returned home, I told Carolyn what the Lord had spoken to me. Then I thought, the only people I know of who are instrumental in missions and who are effective in going to the nations are T.L. and Daisy Osborn. So I made arrangements to go to their ministry headquarters in Tulsa.

When I arrived, I asked one of the staff members who greeted me if the ministry had any material on the Osborn crusades and any books I could purchase to take home and study. The staff member showed me what the Osborns had available, including newsletters that talked about the results of their crusades. I purchased anything I thought might help direct me.

Then someone said, "By the way, we have some of the crusades from Africa and India on film. Would you like to see them?"

I answered yes, and then I was ushered into a room where I had the privilege of watching films of T.L. and Daisy Osborn ministering to masses of people. I was overwhelmed by the size of the crowds, the anointing on the Osborns, and the miracles that took place. I could see why they were referred to as the pioneers of mass-miracle evangelism, and yet what touched me most was their genuine love for people.

Compassion for the Lost

If somebody were to ask me what one thing about T.L. Osborn most impacted my life, I would have to say it was his compassion for the lost. Both he and Daisy wanted people to know their Jesus, and they wanted them to experience His love and His power.

When I left the Osborn headquarters that day, I sensed my own compassion for the lost and a heart for missions like I'd never had before. Over the next few years as I prayed about the continent of Africa, and Kenya in particular, I endeavored to get my hands on anything concerning the Osborns' ministry that showed me how they conducted their overseas crusades.

Then in 1978, the time came for me to make my very first trip to Kenya. I didn't know anyone there, but I'd received a letter from a national there, a young minister. He told me he had gone to an Assembly of God conference in Nairobi in search of someone who could help him with his outreach in the bush. (The bush is a rural area where people live in mud huts with no electricity and no running water.)

The young man said he had approached minister after minister, asking, "Will you help us? Will you help us?" But either they didn't sense the leading of the Lord, or they were not capable of helping. Finally he went to one man who told him, "I can't help you, but the man you are looking for is Jerry Savelle."

Now, to this day I have no idea who the man was that told the young minister to look for me, but when I got the minister's letter telling me the story, I considered it my confirmation that it was time to go to Kenya. I didn't know any other way of doing missions other than what I'd seen T.L. Osborn do. So I sent the money in advance for the young minister to arrange crusades in four cities.

When I arrived and set my feet on African soil for the very first time, I felt the compassion of God come upon me. At that moment, before I even met one person, I fell in love with the continent of Africa as I heard the Lord speak these words to me: "Kenya is your springboard to the African continent. You will fall in love with the people here, and it will happen everywhere you go on this continent."

When I got through customs, the young Kenyan minister was waiting for me. He took me immediately to the city of Nakuru, which was quite a distance from the airport. The next day we got into a little truck with attached external speakers that were almost as big as the truck. We drove throughout the village and rural areas, announcing in Swahili that a movie would be shown that night. My host explained that people in the rural areas had nothing to do at night, and they loved movies. So the way to gather a crowd was to announce a movie night. My host went on to say that the movie being shown that night was a T.L. Osborn crusade.

Mass-Miracle Evangelism

When I arrived at the open-air crusade area that night, I was astonished at the number of people who had gathered. The scene was like those I'd seen in the Osborn films, the only difference being that the Osborn crusades drew hundreds of thousands and I had only drawn thousands. I was nonetheless thrilled that so many had come out for the first Savelle crusade conducted in a foreign country.

I'd learned from watching Brother Osborn's films that a simple message was the most powerful message. So I began preaching a simple message about Jesus, declaring that He was the oppression breaker. Miracles started to happen while I was preaching. In fact, they were occurring so rapidly that I had to quit preaching so that people could testify of what Jesus was doing. I was living the modern-day version of Mark 16:20: "And they went out and preached everywhere, the Lord working with them and confirming the word with the accompanying signs."

Every time someone would testify, another miracle would happen. And so it went for I don't know how long. Later when I gave the invitation, hundreds of people came forward to receive the Lord. I was there for three nights, and then I moved on to the next city, and then the next.

The realization that God had called me to foreign soil where miracles were happening and hundreds were coming to Christ was making a tremendous impact on my life. And yet something was not right. I sensed what I was doing was not exactly what God had called me to do in the continent of Africa. T.L. Osborn was already doing a phenomenal job evangelizing. So what, exactly, did God want Jerry Savelle to do?

After seeking God's direction in prayer, I realized He wanted to use the teaching gift that had come upon me for the purpose of discipling the African nationals. So, rather than continuing with the crusades, I rented a small church in one of the villages. I thought if I could get eighty pastors grounded in the Word of God, we could take the nation. Discipleship became my mission.

At the Lord's direction, we gathered eighty pastors and brought them to the church where I spoke to them multiple times throughout the day. I still conducted evening services where the Lord continued to confirm His Word with miracles. People were saved by the hundreds, but my primary focus was teaching the Word of God.

It was so exciting to watch people who had never been *taught* the Word of God as they learned the principles of faith and the reality of their covenant with God. They grabbed hold of covenant teaching faster than anyone I'd ever seen; they were tribespeople who already had an understanding of covenant.

The first week I was there, I drilled into them the fact that they were the seed of Abraham, and because they were the seed of Abraham, they were entitled to the same blessings of Abraham because of his covenant with God.

I told them, "I will keep coming to teach the Word of God, but you will never hear me refer to you as third-world people. You are the seed of Abraham. If the covenant will work for me, it will also work for you. God is not an American, and Americans did not write the Bible."

Seeing lives changed in Africa has been a great blessing to me over the years. I am always mindful that it was the inspiration of T.L. and Daisy Osborn's mass-miracle crusades that drew me into the ongoing work of discipleship that continues today.

A Love for the Nations

Although I'd not yet met T.L. and Daisy Osborn, just being exposed to their teaching and watching their films was what allowed God's love for the nations to be deposited into me.

There were times when I'd go to a particular nation and I'd call Carolyn at home to say, "I've fallen in love with this nation and its people."

She would always say, "Jerry, you fall in love with the people of every nation you go to."

And she was right. It would just happen

The first time I went to Singapore, Carolyn was with me. I fell in love with the people. The first time I went to Ukraine, I fell in love with the people. The first time I went to Australia, I fell in love with the people. Even when I went to a nation that was under Communist control, I fell in love with the people.

I believe this love for the nations came through a direct impartation I received by watching and studying T.L. and Daisy Osborn.

It was not until 1981 that I actually had the opportunity to meet this amazing couple. I was preaching in Kenneth Hagin's Tulsa campmeeting and was scheduled to start the morning service that day. Brother Hagin introduced me, and when I stepped to the podium and faced the crowd, there were T.L. and Daisy Osborn sitting on the first row right in front of me. I was shocked. Here were two of my faith heroes whom I'd never met, sitting just feet from me as I was about to preach. I felt so honored to be in the same building with these two great apostles.

When I finished the morning's message, I turned the service back to Brother Hagin and then went to the back of the platform and down the stairs to the main floor. Standing there waiting for me were T.L. and Daisy Osborn.

They introduced themselves and said, "We came today to ask if you and your wife would come to our home and spend the afternoon with us."

I said, "Are you serious? You want Carolyn and me to come to your home for the afternoon?"

"Yes," they said.

I could hardly believe what was happening. But what an afternoon it was! They talked about the goodness of God, His compassion for the lost, and His heart for missions. Brother Osborn told us about their crusades, what they had seen in their years of ministry together, and how they got started.

I'd read their books and already knew most of the factual information, but hearing them talk about how God had called them into the ministry of mass-miracle evangelism was uplifting and encouraging. "Brother Jerry," Brother Osborn said, "our number one job is evangelism." Those words went deep into my heart, and they still motivate me today.

Then he took us into his office and said, "Sit in my chair, Brother Savelle." As I sat in T.L. Osborn's chair behind his desk, I remember saying to the Lord, "Let everything that is on him get on me."

Next he took us to the museum that was part of their ministry headquarters. They had collected artifacts from all over the world, wherever they had conducted a crusade. Every piece had a story. There were items that witchdoctors had given them after they'd been saved and delivered. There was even a shrunken head from one of the tribes that had practiced head shrinking before coming to the Lord. It was an amazing museum, and every piece had a story. Each time we would walk by an item, Brother Osborn would remember something that had happened in the corresponding crusade. And his stories were always so uplifting. It was as if Jesus Himself were talking to us, telling of all the miracles and deliverances that had taken place.

After we saw the museum, Brother Osborn said, "I heard you like antique automobiles. Would you like to see my cars?"

I said, "Yes, sir, I would love to."

I followed him into a room that had the most exclusive antique Lincoln collection in the world. He had more antique Lincolns than anyone else at that time. One of them was a model that had been custom-built, and Brother Osborn had somehow managed to acquire it and place it in the museum. It was a 1932, pearl-white Lincoln Roadster convertible.

"Come sit on the running board with me," he said. So I joined him on the running board, and he began to pour into me the wisdom of God regarding missions and how to reach the nations. My life was significantly impacted that day.

A lot has changed in my life and ministry since 1981, but one thing that hasn't changed is my love for the nations that was imparted into me by T.L. Osborn.

Tranquility Produces Creativity

Just before we left the museum that afternoon, he asked me, "Do you know why I surround myself with all of this?"

"No, sir, I don't."

"Because God taught me years ago that if I would surround myself with things that bring peace, I would always be creative." He paused and then said, "Jerry, if you're going to be involved in missions, you've got to be creative. Tranquility produces creativity."

I knew he was right. I'd heard Oral Roberts say it like this: "Don't ever get married to methods. God may have you do something a certain way for a season, but then He may change the method. So you've got to be creative, and in God's ministries, you've got to be creative."

Carolyn and I left T.L. and Daisy Osborn that afternoon with our faith high and energized. Not only that, but we were also dreaming new dreams. I could now see myself on the mission field doing things I'd never dreamed I would do.

Daisy told Carolyn, "If you like the sound of water, get a waterfall. If the sound of a waterfall brings you peace, then surround yourself with them. Every time you experience peace, that tranquility will produce creativity."

If you go to our house today, you'll see that we have waterfalls. And if you go to my shop, you'll see cars there. None of these things are our source of peace; that comes from the Holy Ghost. But He does sometimes use old cars and motorcycles to bring peace to my life.

I can be in my shop working on an old car, and that's when I'll start hearing from God. I used to tell Carolyn, "I know you may not believe this, but God rides that motorcycle with me. I hear God every time I get on that bike."

She would say, "Jerry, you just like riding motorcycles."

"I'm serious, God likes riding them too!" And as long as I maintain the legal speed, He stays on the bike with me.

We learned about tranquility and creativity from T.L. Osborn. In fact, when we recently finished building my dream garage, I named one room the T.L. Osborn room because everything in it is something that brings me peace and tranquility.

I've learned the world doesn't want us to have anything; religion doesn't want us to have nice things. There are lots of people who certainly don't want us to have anything. And yet T.L. Osborn, one of the greatest preachers of his time, took Carolyn and me to another level. He said, "God made all things. All things were made by and for Him. As long as you keep Him first place in your life, He doesn't mind blessing you with all the things that bring peace in your life."

Carolyn and I took to heart what we learned from T.L. and Daisy Osborn, and we've surrounded ourselves with the things that bring us peace. That's why we both remain creative. I hear God when I walk in my study or I'm working in my shop.

Years ago when I told Carolyn I would one day build a shop for my cars, she said, "Quit calling it a shop. It's going to be a museum."

So I said, "One of these days I'm going to build a museum with all my classic cars and have a desk right in the middle where I can just look at them and hear from God." And that's exactly what I have today. It's such a blessing to hear from God as I sit at my desk in my classic car museum.

The articles I've chosen for my study wouldn't make sense to an interior designer. I love studying World War II. I guess you could say I'm a World War II buff. Many of the articles brought back from that war by my dad, Carolyn's dad, and our uncles are proudly displayed in my study.

I'm also proud of my American Indian heritage. I have various headdresses and artifacts that I've been given by members of the Navajo and Cherokee tribes I've been privileged to preach to. When I walk into my study and look at all of those cherished items, it brings peace to me. And I am always creative, because I'm always hearing from God.

I also believe this peace has helped me have a proper sense of timing related to making changes. I know when it's time to do things differently; I know when to change. I believe this sense of timing comes as a result of the peace I experience through surrounding myself with those things that bring peace.

I am thankful for the wisdom T.L. Osborn shared with me that day in his museum as we were surrounded by the things that brought him tranquility and which served as evidence of the creativity that tranquility had produced.

Uplift and Encourage

On one of the occasions I had to spend time with Brother Osborn, he said to me, "Brother Jerry, don't ever preach down to people. Lift people up every time you preach. Don't ever say 'ouch' words to people."

"Brother Osborn, what are ouch words?" I asked.

"Words that hurt or words that wound. Don't ever say things that pull people down," he explained. Then he put his hand on my shoulder and said, "You have a gift, and that gift is encouraging people and lifting them up. Always go to the pulpit depending on that gift." That's when he started calling me the smart preacher.

I remember one time when I landed at the Dallas/Fort Worth International Airport. I was walking through the terminal when I saw T.L. and Daisy Osborn standing in front of a monitor, looking for their gate number. They hadn't seen me, so I just walked up behind and said, "Could I help you people find your gate?"

As he was turning toward me Brother Osborn said, "We're looking for the gate for . . . Oh, look, Daisy, it's the smart preacher!" I asked him why he called me the smart preacher. He said, "Because you are a great communicator, and you have a gift of lifting people up."

He also had a phrase he used all the time. "Oh boy, oh wow," he would say to express his delight and encouragement. There was never a time when I was in his presence that he wasn't encouraging me. He would say, "Oh boy, oh wow. You're so great. You're so smart."

I remember when Evelyn Roberts went home to be with the Lord,

Carolyn and I were there along with both of our daughters. When I saw Brother Osborn there with his daughter, LaDonna, on his arm, I walked up and tapped him on the shoulder. "Brother Osborn, my family and I just wanted to say hello to you."

He turned around and said, "Oh, LaDonna, it's the smart preacher. Oh boy, you're so smart. You're so wonderful. I just love you." When I introduced him to my girls, he said, "Oh boy, your dad is so smart. He is so great. He's so wonderful."

Although I didn't have the opportunity to spend as much time with T.L. Osborn as I did with Kenneth Copeland, Oral Roberts, and Kenneth Hagin, the impact he made on my life and ministry was nonetheless significant. I count it a great honor to have had the privilege of knowing this great apostle of God.

7

Harold Nichols

Although he wasn't world renowned, Harold Nichols was one of the greatest men of God I've ever known. He was my pastor for many, many years.

I've often said there are men of God and there are godly men, but Harold Nichols was both. And that's not something I can say about every preacher I meet. I used to tell Brother Nichols all the time, "When I grow up I want to be jut like you, only with hair." Harold Nichols was one of my faith heroes who pastored for over sixty years before he went home to be with the Lord at age ninety-three. He and his wife, Lou, were married for over seventy years.

While we were still living in Shreveport, Harold Nichols was one of the first pastors who invited me to come preach at his church, Grace Temple. Of course, Kenneth Copeland had encouraged Brother Nichols to do so, because he didn't know me at the time. Brother Copeland told him how involved I was in soul winning and street evangelism, so Brother Nichols invited me to come to his church and conduct a youth meeting.

Well, we got his youth organized and took them out in the streets where they had great success winning other young people to Christ. I preached at the youth service one Wednesday evening, and Harold and Lou were there. Years later, Lou told me that when they got home after the youth service, she said to Harold, "That boy needs to keep working on cars. He's not a good preacher."

Brother Nichols said, "Now, Lou, you just give him time. That boy's got something."

After I moved to Fort Worth to work for Brother Copeland, they would invite me from time to time to preach at their church. The first time I preached at an adult service, Lou again said, "I still think that boy needs to go back to working on cars."

But Brother Harold said, "I'm telling you, Lou, that boy's got something. You just watch; God's going to use him."

Finally, God did indeed start using me just as Brother Nichols had said. That's when Lou began to say to me, "Brother Jerry, you're one of the best. You're one of my favorite teachers." Then she would get right in my face and say, "Now don't you ever change!" Even when I was sixty years old, she'd tell me, "You be the same sweet little boy you've always been."

Harold Nichols took a common-sense approach to ministry, which is one of the reasons he continued to pastor for six decades. I believe his longevity was a result of three specific principles he taught me by both word and example.

First, never lose your love for serving God. For Brother Nichols, serving God wasn't his job; it was his life. He was a carpenter when, in the late 40s or early 50s, he heard the call of God to preach. So he built a church with his own hands and began preaching. For the next sixty years he did the two things he loved most: he worked with his hands, and he served God. Brother Harold particularly loved to help others build churches because doing so allowed him to enjoy doing what he loved. He kept building churches until he couldn't climb a ladder anymore, but he never stopped serving God. He counted it a great honor that God would call him into the ministry. I can remember him saying to me, "Brother Jerry, don't ever lose your love for serving God."

Second, never lose your compassion for hurting people. Brother Nichols was the kind of pastor who, if he heard you had so much as a fever, was there at your side ready to pray for you. He loved people, and he loved to help people. This is the heart of a real pastor. He would tell me, "Brother Jerry, I know you're busy, and I know you have a lot of things to do, but don't ever get to the place where some of these preachers get, where they don't have compassion for hurting people. Always remember, ministry is about helping people."

And *third,* don't ever lose your joy. One of the characteristics I enjoyed most about Brother Nichols when I was around him was he was almost always whistling, humming, or singing an old hymn. He was always a man of joy. I remember going to his home at times when he'd be up on a ladder nailing shingles or performing some sort of task. As I approached, I'd always hear some joyful tune emanating from him. I remember asking Lou one day if he did that all the time. She said, "All the time. Not just when people can hear him. Not just when he's around church people. He does it all the time." And until the day he went home to be with the Lord, he never lost his joy.

Harold Nichols not only preached these principles, he lived them. I've seen many preachers over the years who have lost their joy. As a result, ministry becomes mechanical; it's just a job, an obligation. But it was not so with Harold Nichols.

There were times when he would share with me problems he experienced with some of the people in his church. I'd ask, "Why do you even want to deal with people who are so hateful and mean?"

And he would say, "Oh now, Brother Jerry, they just don't know any better." Harold Nichols would just love them and help them and minister to them.

I watched him pour his life into people, only to have them turn around and stab him in the back. But he would never say anything ugly about them. The most he'd say was, "Well, they're going to another church now. I did all I could for them, so I hope their new pastor can help them and take them to another level."

Harold Nichols remained joyful and never lost his love of serving God or his compassion for hurting people. That's a great way to approach ministry, and I will always be grateful for what I learned from this very special man who was my pastor, my mentor, and my friend.

8

Dave Malkin

Dave Malkin was the man God used to teach me how to become a one-on-one soul winner. After my father-in-law introduced me to Kenneth Copeland and he learned what I was doing in the streets of Shreveport, he said, "I know a man in California who does the very same thing, but he's taken it to another level, and I want you to go out there and spend as much time as you need so that he can teach you what he's learned about evangelism." So Brother Copeland paid my way to go to Los Angeles to meet Dave Malkin.

I learned that David Smith Malkin was a successful businessman. He was a landscape architect who was active in the Full Gospel Business Men's Fellowship and served on the board of Campus Crusade for Christ. He was also a great soul winner.

The charismatic movement had just begun at that time, and Dave was right out there in California where the hippie movement, with all its wildness and perversion, was in full swing. When I arrived in California, I realized that our so-called hippies back in Louisiana were just a bunch of wannabes; they had no clue about the lifestyle these West Coast hippies were living.

The love Dave Malkin had for the lost was amazing. Although he had a business to run, not a day passed when he wasn't out sharing Jesus in the streets, parks, malls, restaurants, gas stations, and everywhere else he went. I never saw a person who came into Dave's presence that he failed to witness to.

By the time I arrived in Los Angeles just prior to the Fourth of July, Dave had assembled a group of 113 young people, most of whom he'd led to the Lord. He had them in his home once a week and was teaching them the Word of God. The plan was to take these 113 new believers to Pismo Beach where over 100,000 hippies would be gathered for the weekend celebration, and invade hell's beachfront outpost with the Word of God.

Nothing Can Stand Against the Love of Christ

When we arrived at our destination, I found myself looking at a sea of humanity that had absolutely no resemblance to me. Here I was, and average guy with a crew cut, dressed in jeans and a pullover shirt, looking at what might as well have been a different species of beings. I didn't look like them, I didn't know their lifestyle, and I didn't know what I could possibly say to reach these people. Many of them were so stoned, they were crawling down the beach—and even in the streets—like wild animals. Some had hair that was so long in both the front and back that I couldn't tell if they were coming or going. One thing I knew for sure: I wasn't in Louisiana anymore.

Dave sensed my apprehension. He said to me, "Your knowledge of their lifestyle isn't important. It's your love for Christ that will reach them. Just tell them about Jesus." And so I did. I'm not sure exactly how many people our little army of 113 led to the Lord that weekend, but it could well have been thousands. We even got to baptize some of them in the Pacific Ocean before we left.

We were about a hundred miles out of Pismo Beach on our way back to Los Angeles when we needed to stop for gas. The attendant came up to our vehicle and said, "Man, have you guys heard what happened at Pismo Beach this weekend?"

We said, "What?"

"They're calling it the Jesus Movement. They baptized hundreds of people in the Pacific Ocean!"

He had no idea he was talking to the very people God had used to make that happen. Nor did he know the man who'd had the vision for it, Dave Malkin, was sitting right there in the car. Dave said, "Well, what about you?" And right then and there, he led that attendant to the Lord.

People Are Waiting for Our Testimony

I ate at my very first Denny's restaurant when I was with Dave Malkin in California. And before we walked out of the place, he had led every server to the Lord. This happened everywhere he went. The apostle Paul said he was a debtor to every man (see Romans 1:14), and that is the way Dave felt. His life had been changed by Jesus, and he felt an obligation to take Jesus to every person he came in contact with.

Dave Malkin taught me God has placed people in our path who are waiting for our testimony. Although I'd already been preaching in the streets of my home city of Shreveport, Dave helped me overcome any trace of lingering timidity when talking to a total stranger. When I got back to Shreveport, I was a witnessing machine. I'd witness to anything that moved.

I started teaching the young people in our church what I'd learned from Dave Malkin, and pretty soon we were winning people all over our city to Christ. Some of the biggest drug addicts and dealers were coming to our house to get delivered—all because of the impartation I received from Dave Malkin.

As my ministry grew throughout the years, I'd have Dave come and teach in our Bible school. Sometimes I'd have him come to one of our crusades and organize a group of people to witness in the street before the meetings. And he made a tremendous impact on our Chariots of Light Christian Bikers Club events. He demonstrated to our members that we are not merely on a motorcycle tour; we are first and foremost evangelists. Even today, Bill and Ginger Horn, our COL International Directors, have the same spirit that was on Dave Malkin: they witness to anything that moves—and if it doesn't move, they just might raise it from the dead to witness to it.

For every soul this ministry has won to the Lord, some of the credit goes to Dave Malkin. It was this great soul winner in California who imparted to me an anointing that is still operating in this ministry today.

God has placed some great men in my life who have imparted to me Bible truths and godly principles that have guided my life and ministry for the past forty-five years, allowing me to impact the lives of hundreds of thousands of people throughout the world.

While I was privileged to have personal relationships with each of the people featured in this book, much of what was imparted to me came from fellowshiping with them through their books and other teaching materials. It is my prayer that now, in turn, the transforming truths and principles I've shared in this book will be a guiding force in your life and ministry, just as they have been in mine.

Photo Gallery

Me, Carolyn, Brother Copeland, Gloria, Oretha, Brother Hagin, and our dear friends, Happy and Jeanne Caldwell, at my 30th year ministry anniversary celebration.

Me and Brother Copeland in the Charlotte, NC, East Coast Believers Convention in 1981.

My pastor, Brother Harold Nichols, preaching at one of my Missions Conferences in the early 80s.

Brother Roberts and me at one of my Revival Fires Conferences.

Brother Osborn speaking at Brother Copeland's Ministers Conference.

95

Me, Carolyn, Oretha, and Brother Hagin during my 30 year ministry celebration in 1999.

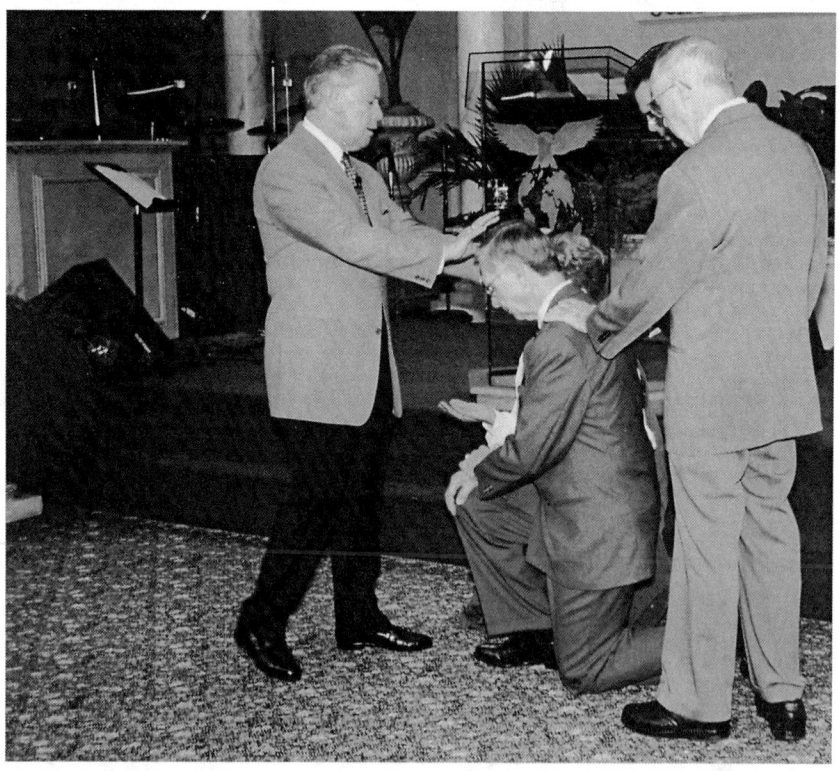

Ordaining and receiving Dave Malkin into our Heritage of Faith Ministerial Association in 2002.

Me, Brother Copeland, and Brother Roberts during the Southwest Believers Convention in Forth Worth, Texas.

Jan and Dave Malkin—a very special couple in my life.

Dave Malkin, me, Brother Copeland, and my son-in-law, Rodney Foy, during my Thunder Over Texas Rally at Texas Motor Speedway.

Brother Copeland and me during the Southwest Believers Convention in the late 90s.

Gloria, Brother Copeland, me, Carolyn, Brother Roberts, and Evelyn during one of my Revival Fires Conferences.

Brother Osborn in one of his powerful crusades.

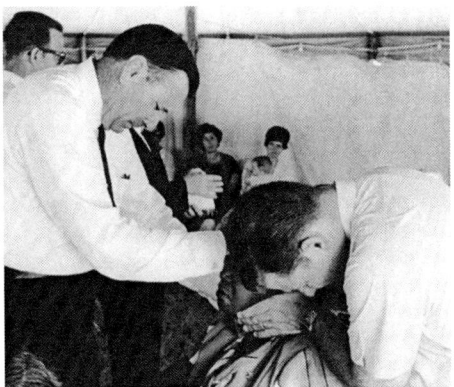

Brother Roberts praying for the sick in one of the great Tent Crusades during the 1950s.

99

Brother Copeland and me during one of his Believers Conventions in the 1990s.

Hilton and JoAnn Sutton, Brother Osborn, me and Carolyn, Dodie and John Osteen, Norvel Hayes, and Gloria in the 1982 Southwest Believers Convention.

Oral Roberts and his famous plaque. A fitting phrase for a man who was known as a big thinker.

Me and Brother Copeland in his Believers Convention in 1981.

Brother Copeland and me during a television taping session for his Believers Voice of Victory program.

Lou, Brother Nichols, and me in our 1994 Missions Conference.

Brother Roberts praying for people during a service at Eagle Mountain International Church.

Brother Copeland ministering at one of his Believers Conventions.

Brother Copeland speaking at my Thunder Over Texas Motorcycle Rally.

103

A Conversation with Jerry and Carolyn Savelle

In the main body of this book I focused on the six men whose lives and ministries made the greatest impact on my life and ministry. But this narrative would not be complete without detailing the roles each of their wives played, not only in the lives and ministries of their husbands, but in making an impact on Carolyn and me as well.

We recently had a conversation about the six extraordinary couples who imparted their love, wisdom, and anointing into our lives, helping to enable us in fulfilling God's call to take His Word to the nations. Carolyn and I are sharing this conversation with the assurance that you, too, will receive an impartation of that same love, wisdom, and anointing.

Kenneth and Gloria Copeland

Carolyn: Jerry has often said, "Beautiful are the feet of those that bring good news or glad tidings." The Copelands' feet will always be considered beautiful in the Savelle household.

When I think of Kenneth and Gloria Copeland, my heart overflows with gratitude. Early in our marriage, Jerry and

What I Learned *from the men who imparted into me the most*

I were two struggling kids who had nothing, who knew nothing. We had two little children of our own, and it seems we were always sick and we were always broke. When I watch our home videos from that time, I can see all the medicine bottles lined up in the windowsill. I think of those days of just struggling and just existing. But when the word of faith came, when truth came, things changed.

I'll never forget the first sermon I heard Brother Copeland preach. His message was entitled "What Happened from the Cross to the Throne." When I heard that sermon, Jesus became real to me. He was no longer a Bible character. He actually was a man who shed His blood on that cross, who died and was buried. On the third day, He was resurrected so that I could live a victorious life. Until then, I never knew anything about living a victorious life.

Jerry: To me, the story of Jesus was just a Christmas story. It was something people talked about at Christmas. I believed Jesus was the Son of God, and I believed He died and was raised from the dead. Yet the nativity was still a Christmas story that really didn't apply to everyday life. But the day we heard Brother Copeland's message, my concept changed.

Carolyn: When Brother Copeland said Jesus hung on the cross, he actually stretched out his arms and turned his back to the audience. He said, "That's what God did to His own Son. He turned His back on Jesus so that He could pay the penalty for Adam's sin." Those words went into my spirit man and into my heart. Jesus actually bore my punishment for me.

Jerry: That's why He cried out, "My God, my God, why hast thou forsaken me?" In other words, that turning away had to take place; God literally had to look upon His Son as sin. The Bible says, "For He made Him who knew no sin to be sin for us, that we might become the righteousness of God in Him" (2 Corinthians 5:21). If Jesus had not been willing to become sin, even though He had never sinned, we could never have experienced God's redemption.

Carolyn: That understanding is what totally changed my life. So the Copelands' feet will be beautiful in the Savelle household forever.

There are other facets of Brother Copeland's character that just touched my heart. He's such a man of faith, he lives a life a faith. He's full of love and full of compassion. But one thing that so touches me is that he's quick to forgive if he is offended. He's also quick to ask for forgiveness if he's offended someone.

A group of us had been together in a meeting with him, and we were going to fly back to Fort Worth together in his airplane. Before we left, he had an appointment with someone regarding a business matter for the ministry. The results of that meeting did not meet his expectations. In fact, the news he got was both unexpected and disappointing.

So, by the time he boarded the airplane to fly us home, he was not happy. He just wasn't nice to be around. But in just a matter of minutes the Holy Spirit arrested him for the way he was behaving. Brother Copeland was so quick to turn to everyone and say, "I'm sorry. I've not been nice. I want to ask all of you to forgive me for being rude this morning. None of you deserve to be talked to and treated the way I've treated you."

His words and actions that day made a significant impact on me because this great man of God was so quick to repent and ask for our forgiveness. I saw firsthand the power of forgiveness, faith, compassion, and love in operation in his life.

Another thing that so impressed me was his giving.

Jerry: Giving became a lifestyle for us as a result of watching Kenneth and Gloria, and the way they gave.

Carolyn: It became a way of life for us. We don't hoard over our checkbook. We get up every day asking God, "What can we do? What can we give? Who can we bless today?"

When I think about Gloria Copeland, I remember something Evelyn Roberts wrote in her autobiography. She said, "Oral Roberts, an uncommon man, needed an uncommon wife." It takes a special woman to be with a man who does what God has called him to do, especially when it involves international exposure and notoriety.

Gloria Copeland is an uncommon wife. This lady was a tremendous influence for both of us. She was, and still is, in the Word day and night. The Word is what is most important to her. In every situation in life, she wants to know what the Word has to say about it. The Word is first place in her life.

Gloria's first book, *God's Will for Your Life*, has helped millions of people understand that Jesus became our substitute in every area so that we can live an overcoming life. He became sickness so that we can be healed. He became poor so that we can have prosperity.

I believe one of the reasons Gloria is so powerful is she dedicates one hour a day to prayer.

Jerry: The first part of her day, every day.

Carolyn: In giving the first part of her day to the Lord, she is actually tithing her time. I've done this all my life. Before I even get out of bed in the morning, I'm lying there quietly, praying and dedicating myself to the Lord. It's something I learned from my mother while I was growing up.

Jerry: Gloria made a great impact on both of us, especially when it came to learning to believe God for our needs. In the early days, we watched her believe God for her home and for every piece of furniture that went in it. We watched Brother Copeland believe for every vehicle they drove, and later for every airplane the ministry owned. We also saw that every time they were ready to believe God to meet a particular need, they first sowed a seed. This was something they learned from Oral Roberts, the miracle of seed faith.

Oral and Evelyn Roberts

Carolyn: When you and I first married, Oral Roberts was on TV all the time, so I wrote for the gifts they offered for free. The first gift that came was a bumper sticker that said Expect a Miracle. We stuck that sticker on our refrigerator because, honestly, we had to expect a miracle in order to have food in our home! That saying made a significant impression on me. But he also taught us the principle of seedtime and harvest.

Jerry: I remember how excited I was when he offered a free book. I said, "Carolyn, we can afford this one. Order it!"

Carolyn: That book, *The Miracle of Seed Faith,* made such an impact on us. What changed our lives was what we learned about the law of seedtime and harvest. Brother Roberts showed us that every seed produces after its own kind and God would honor our faith when we sowed. We discovered we could plant one little seed and know we were going to get a whole crop, a whole harvest on it.

When we came to know Oral and Evelyn Roberts, they were older and had become fully developed and focused on the biblical truths they'd established in their lives. Because they were so seasoned, we felt like they were spiritual grandparents to us. And as we've learned, grandchildren almost always have funny stories they can tell about their grandparents.

Back when it was stylish for women to wear a long hairpiece that was called a fall, Oral and Evelyn came to stay with us in our home for a few days. The fall I wore at the time was long and curly, and I made sure it was carefully pinned in place each morning before I left our bedroom.

The first day they were with us, Brother Roberts walked up to me, patted my hair, and said to his wife, "Evelyn, look at this little angel's hair. That's the most beautiful hair I've ever seen." He did the same thing each morning for the next three days. On the final night they were with us, as he was telling me how pretty my hair was, I said, "Brother Roberts, you've enjoyed my hair so much for the past three days that I want you to have it." Then I reached up and removed my fall, handed it to him, and said, "Here, why don't you wear it?"

Without a word, he took the hairpiece, placed it on his head, and then walked over to the mirror. He patted it and looked at himself from every angle, and then he asked Evelyn, "What do you think about my hair? Isn't this wonderful?" He was hilarious. But instead of returning my fall, he wore it into his bedroom, and I didn't see it again until the next morning.

Jerry: I bet there's not another person in the world that can share that testimony. Another time they were in our home I told them before we all went to bed, "Make yourself at home. Our home is your home." I got up the next morning to make Evelyn coffee, because she had told me "Oral, doesn't make good coffee. I love your coffee." When I walked into the kitchen, Brother Roberts was there with his back to me, standing in front of the open refrigerator, his hair sticking up all over his head.

I always keep a water bottle in there for myself, and he had the water bottle—*my* water bottle—and he was drinking from it. Then he got the milk carton and took a big drink out of it. About that time he turned and saw me. "Well, you told me to make myself at home and this is the way I do it at home," he said. I thought, what a prized moment. I don't know if anybody else can say Oral Roberts drank milk out of the milk carton at their house.

Oral and Evelyn were down-to-earth people who made an impact all over the world with their strong faith. He laid his hands on over a million people during his years in ministry, and yet they were very ordinary people in many ways.

I remember his son Richard said this to me after they left our home: "I don't know what you did for Mom and Dad, but they have been raving about what a great time they had in your home." Brother Roberts and Evelyn both said, "We haven't stayed in people's homes in a long, long time, but this time has restored our confidence."

Carolyn: Oral and Evelyn Roberts were loved by many people throughout the world, but they were also severely criticized. I remember sitting with Evelyn one day as she talked about that criticism. She told me what it was like to raise the children of a famous father—how they had to face the jeers, the slurring, and being made fun of at school. Through tears, she also talked of losing not only two of those children but also a son-in-law.

    We got to see the vulnerable human side of this great couple, but we also saw the overcoming, victorious side. We saw how tragic events didn't cause them to stop doing what God had called them to do. We saw the compassion and the love of God rise up big on the inside of them. And we watched as they picked themselves up and carried on in the Word of God.

Jerry: The example they set has been such a blessing to us, especially where it concerns family. When we had issues in our own family, I would always remember how Oral and Evelyn handled their most difficult circumstances. When we followed their example, we got the same victorious results. God would always bless us, even in the midst of tragedy.

Carolyn: Another important thing we learned from Brother Roberts was the need for ministers to rest. For years and years, we went on vacation with two other couples: Buddy and Pat Harrison, and Happy and Jeanne Caldwell. When we would go down to the pool, we were supposed to be resting, relaxing, and having a good time. But for a number of those years, everybody brought study materials and study books down to the pool. Finally, Buddy said, "We've got to stop this. We can't bring study materials down to the pool anymore. We've come to rest, and that's what we're going to do." So Brother Roberts helped you in that area, didn't he?

Jerry: Yes, he did. He once told me he studied and prayed so much, and was involved in meetings so much, that he finally realized he needed a change of pace. So he started reading Louis L'Amour Western novels as a recreational pastime.

Well, he got me to reading those Westerns too. Years later we were at a Marriott hotel, and I was lying around the pool reading a Louis L'Amour book. I looked up and recognized the two men walking by me: Louis L'Amour and Bill Marriott. Louis looked down at me and saw I was reading one of his books, and he winked at me. I was so taken aback at seeing the author of my book in front of me that I didn't have a chance to ask him to autograph it!

Whether it was biblical principals or the application of practical truths, the things Oral and Evelyn Roberts imparted into our lives defy monetary value. They're still impacting me. And I'm still doing things today, both in my personal life and in my ministry, that I learned from Oral Roberts.

Kenneth and Oretha Hagin

Carolyn: When I think of Brother Hagin, of course I think of Mark 11:23–24: "For assuredly, I say to you, whoever says to this mountain, 'Be removed and be cast into the sea,' and does not doubt in his heart, but believes that those things he says will be done, he will have whatever he says. Therefore I say to you, whatever things you ask when you pray, believe that you receive them, and you will have them."

When that scripture became revelation on the inside of

us, it changed our lives. Our daughter Terri's fingers had just been cut off when we first heard Brother Hagin teach that scripture just days later. As a result of our doing what Mark 11:23–24 says, we received a miracle. Terri's fingers grew back and became normal. What a mighty God we serve.

Jerry: Following the accident, we kept confessing and saying, "Our God will restore our baby's fingers." We believed this in our hearts and never doubted.

Carolyn: Brother Hagin was so in tune with God and in tune with the Holy Spirit. He flowed in the gifts of the Spirit like nobody we had ever seen before. But he also had a playful side to his personality.

His daughter, Pat Harrison, asked me to come to Tulsa to redecorate her daughter's bedroom as gift for her. So I flew up there and got to work. I spent my time up on a ladder painting, seated at the sewing machine making drapes, and doing all sorts of other decorating tasks. Brother Hagin would stop by the house every day to check on progress. That was his granddaughter's room and he would come over to check on me. I might be high on that ladder when he got there, and he would take the ladder and shake it and pinch me to make me think I was going to fall off that ladder. He was a real prankster.

Jerry: When Brother Hagin and Oretha were in our home one time, he got to telling stories, like he always did, about what God was doing back in 1948. We were sitting there and just hanging onto every word. Our daughters, Jerriann and Terri, were in third and fourth grade at the time, and the next day was a school day. You told them they needed to go get their pajamas and robes on and get ready for bed. They did what you said, but then they came back to listen to Brother Hagin.

We kept telling them they had to go to school in the morning. It was already past midnight, but they begged and begged. So finally we told them okay. What better thing than to sit there and listen to this great man of God? They lay on the floor on their stomachs with their faces in their hands, looking up and listening to Brother Hagin as he told all those stories.

I remember when he went home to be with Lord, we were going to Tulsa for the homecoming and I asked the girls, "What's your most memorable time with the Hagins?" And that was it. They said, "When you let us sit there and listen to all those stories."

Carolyn: Aren't we glad we let them stay up late?

Jerry: Yes. I can't forget the time he asked me to preach with him in Nashville. It was snowing like crazy, and you and I went out to get in the car with Brother Hagin and Oretha, who were already waiting for us. Brother Hagin got out of the passenger side, and when you walked toward him, he threw a small snowball and hit you right in the face. You bent down to make one, and he ran to the car and locked the door. He wouldn't let us in until you put down that snowball.

On the way back you told him you were going to get him back. We pulled up in front of the hotel, and before the car even stopped, he opened the door and jumped out. He took off running toward the entrance doors of the hotel. You ran out behind him and grabbed a snowball. He opened the door to run inside just as some businessmen were walking out. You threw the snowball, he ducked, and you hit those total strangers. Brother Hagin just fell to his knees and laughed and laughed.

The Hagins made such powerful impartations into us spiritually, which changed our life, but they also let us see their human side. They loved life and they had fun. That's the way we live our life. We are obviously dedicated to the call of God, deeply committed to the preaching of the Word, and meeting the needs of people. But at the same time we have fun. We have our human side.

Carolyn: I want to talk about Oretha Hagin. What a woman. What a powerhouse of God. Here again, she was an uncommon wife for an uncommon man. So many times the wives of ministers are left at home to raise the children while the men are on the road. This was the case with Oretha Hagin. It takes a strong woman to be left at home to deal with all the daily situations.

Mrs. Hagin helped me at a time in my life when I was going through some difficult female issues. I was believing God for my healing, but Pat Harrison told me, "Talk to Mom about this." So I went to Mrs. Hagin, and told her what I was going through and what I was experiencing.

She said, "Carolyn, go to the doctor and see what procedure they recommend for you." I did what she said and then told her what had been recommended. She said, "Carolyn, have that procedure done."

She taught me that going to the doctor was not an indication of a lack of faith; getting medical help did not mean I was a faith failure. She assured me that God would join me at my level of faith. That took the biggest burden of guilt and condemnation off me. I could have this medical procedure done and God wasn't going to hate me because of it or dislike me or disown me for doing it. God was going to join me at my level of faith.

God indeed did join me at my level of faith as I believed that He would guide the surgeon's hands and the procedure would be a success. Sure enough, when I left the hospital, I was a new person. All because Oretha Hagin had such wisdom and compassion, and she was willing to help me.

Jerry: Some people think going to a doctor is the sign of no faith or a lack of faith. No, that's not the way medical help should be viewed. Remember, Luke, one of Jesus' disciples, was a physician. The way I see it, the two can work together.

T.L. and Daisy Osborn

Carolyn: T.L. and Daisy Osborn were special people to me. When I was a little girl growing up in Life Tabernacle Church in Shreveport, they would come to our church. I grew up watching their videos (well, they were slides back then). I saw the miracles they documented: the blind received their sight and the lame stood and walked. I just saw every kind of miracle. To me, the Osborns were people you put up on a pedestal because of the miraculous power of God flowing through them. I never dreamed I would ever meet them or that we would have a relationship with them.

You've repeated so many times the statement Brother Osborn made that changed us forever: "Surround yourself with what brings you joy, and from tranquility comes creativity." I took that advice to heart and surrounded myself with running water.

Jerry: I remember when he told you that. T.L. and Daisy asked us to go to their home with them one time. They said, "If you like waterfalls, if you like the sound of water, have waterfalls and running water all over your property."

Carolyn: I did just that, and from the tranquility they give me, comes creativity. God is so good. Another thing you've pointed out about Brother Osborn is he never spoke ouch words. I need to play that in my mind all the time: don't speak ouch words, but only words that are uplifting and beneficial.

And again, here's another example of an uncommon man with and uncommon wife: Daisy Washburn Osborn. She was one in a million because she was the legs, the arms, the mouth, the feet, the eyes for Brother Osborn. She was the hands behind the whole organization, always working to get the job done.

Jerry: One time when I was in Kenya, I was with a group of nationals, and we were walking down a dusty road. We were headed for a village to conduct a meeting under a brush arbor. On the road ahead of us, I saw Daisy Osborn with about twenty young Kenyan ministers. I walked toward her, and when she realized who I was, she exclaimed, "Brother Savelle!" I asked what she was doing there, and she told me she was preparing for a crusade. I asked if Brother Osborn was with her, and she said, "Oh no, honey, Brother Osborn's at home. He sends me over here six months in advance to get everything set up. I do all the work. He gets all the glory."

They were a wonderful team, and that's a lesson to be learned where ministries are concerned. Husbands and wives are a team. It's not his ministry and she's just the wife, or her ministry and he's just the husband. They are a team. T.L. and Daisy Osborn definitely came across as a God-ordained team.

Carolyn: One of the things about Daisy Osborn that stands out in my mind was her respect for the dignitaries and heads of state and presidents of those nations. She also had high regard for ministers of the gospel. One time we had breakfast with her and Brother Osborn, and Kenneth and Gloria Copeland. When the waiter came to take our order, Brother Copeland wanted his omelet cooked a special way. The waiter said, "I'm sorry, sir, we can't make an omelet that way." Daisy turned to that waiter and said, "Son, do you not know who this is you're talking to? This is the man of God." The young man was just shocked. Then she said, "Would you mind taking me to your chef, please?"

So Daisy got up and went with the waiter into the kitchen to talk to the chef. Minutes later, the chef came out and personally asked Brother Copeland how he would like his omelet cooked. Daisy got that omelet made just the way Brother Copeland wanted, just to honor him as the man of God. So she knew what respect was and what honor was. That made one of the greatest impressions on me.

Jerry: That's the way she was about their ministry. You didn't tell Daisy Osborn something couldn't be done. She would show you that it certainly could. She was a take-charge kind of lady.

Carolyn: I think all these women we've talked about were like that.

Jerry: Although most of them remained in the background, we were privileged to see they were strong women of faith, resolute and determined. They believed in their husbands and each one backed her husband completely.

Harold and Lou Nichols

Carolyn: When I think of Harold and Lou Nichols, I think of joy unspeakable and full of glory. Harold was so full of joy that he hummed and sang all of the time. He even jingled the change in his pockets. He was so full of joy because of his daily, early-morning relationship time with the Lord.

He was just the most amazing man. One of the things that so touched me was the fact that he was a carpenter and he worked with his hands. Jesus was a carpenter, and when I think of Brother Harold Nichols, I think of Jesus, because he was so much like Jesus.

He loved everybody he came in contact with. Being pastors for over fifty years like Harold and Lou were, they taught me this important thing: you have people come and you have people go, but the main thing is, love them while you have them. Brother Nichols said, "They're not going to stay with you forever. Love them when you have them, and when they go, let them go. When they come back and say hi to you, you can continue to love them, but you don't harbor offense in your heart. Just impart into them as much as they will allow you to."

Jerry: Brother Harold was one of the first pastors to believe in us. Brother Copeland once said, "When I first met Jerry Savelle, he had the anointing of a duck. He couldn't preach his way out of a wet paper sack." Of course he believed in me, but he was giving the illustration of how raw I was in the beginning and what God had done with me.

But Harold Nichols was there at the beginning; he and Brother Copeland ordained me. He was there at the beginning and all the way through. Brother Nichols served this ministry and served our board. He and Lou believed in us.

Carolyn: Lou was always one of those get-in-your face kind of women. If she saw you doing something wrong, she would always want to guide you to do it right. She wasn't afraid to tell you exactly how things should be. In the beginning she didn't think you were going to amount to anything, and she told you that. She said, "I had my doubts about you, Brother Jerry."

Jerry: But Brother Nichols kept saying, "Now, Lou, honey, you give him time. He's really got something. It will come out."

Carolyn: That's what he would tell her. But I'm telling you, now you are Lou Nichols' favorite preacher. She thinks you and God hung the moon.

Jerry: She would kiss me and say, "Now Brother Jerry, I know God's using you, but don't you dare change. You stay the nice, sweet man that you are."

Dave and Jan Malkin

Carolyn: I remember Dave Malkin as a soul winner who changed your life in so many ways. I'll never forget when you got home from California after spending time with him; your life was changed forever.

What I Learned *from the men who imparted into me the most*

Jerry: He taught me how to win people one-on-one.

Carolyn: You hit the streets running, winning souls for the Lord. You hadn't even been home a day and there you were, out soul winning.

One of the stories you told me about what happened while you were out there with Dave really made an impression on me. You said you were standing under a streetlight while Dave was witnessing to this man who was hesitant about accepting the Lord, when all of a sudden the streetlight went out.

Jerry: There were several streetlights in the vicinity, but the one we were under was the only one that went out. Dave was so quick to think. The moment the light went out, he said, "Sir, that's how it could be in your life. What if your light went out tonight? Would you know that you would spend eternity with God or not?" That's what woke the man up. He said, "Mister, I don't want my light going out tonight, and I know I don't want to spend eternity in hell. Let's pray."

Dave was so quick to use everything around him as a means to reach into a person's heart. He was the greatest one-on-one evangelist I've ever met in my life.

Carolyn: We had him here year after year to teach in the Bible school. He trained our students every year, and they would go out soul winning. I remember sitting in those classes, and his teaching would so set me on fire that I would go out and do soul winning right along with them. When you were around Dave, your thoughts were on nothing but soul winning.

Jerry: Dave witnessed to everybody in the restaurants where we ate and in the hotels where we stayed. I used to have Dave go into a city ahead of me in my crusades. He would go into churches and recruit people to witness. He would train them, set up teams, and then launch them into the streets several days before I arrived.

One time in Birmingham, Alabama, when I arrived at the hotel, Dave was standing out front witnessing to one of the parking attendants. My dad and your dad were with me, and I said, "Watch guys, that man will have his head bowed in just a few minutes." Well, sure enough, he did. Dave looked up and saw me and said, "Brother Jerry, I want you to meet a new brother in Christ." He introduced us, and we told the guy how happy we were.

The doorman greeted Dave as we entered the lobby, and Dave said, "Oh, Brother Jerry, I got him saved yesterday." We went up to the front desk, and Dave said, "Oh, the manager here got saved yesterday, and the guy that's going to take your luggage up to your room, he got saved too." Dave had won nearly everybody that worked at that hotel to the Lord before I got there.

Carolyn: That was Dave Malkin.

Jerry: Dave's wife, Jan, watched him do this with everybody. I mean with everybody. If it was alive and breathing, he witnessed to it. If it wasn't breathing, he prayed for it, got it to breathe, and then witnessed to it. Jan was by his side day and night, and she was just as excited about the people who came to Christ as he was. I never once heard her say, "Dave, could you let it rest? I'd like to eat without you preaching." She may have, but I never heard it. Jan Malkin was yet another uncommon woman.

Carolyn: I was thinking about our Chariots of Light Christian Bikers Club. This year alone we've had over seventeen thousand salvations. Dave is in heaven now, but we know that some of the credit goes to him for every one of those souls that have been saved—and are still being saved.

Carolyn and I wanted to share some of the more intimate times that we had with these great men and women who've imparted so much into us. As we've already said, they made a tremendous impact on our lives. We are so grateful to God that we were privileged not only to sit under their ministries but also to get to know them personally and to become friends and co-laborers in the Lord.

I am forever grateful that God gave me my precious wife, Carolyn, who has believed in me all these years. She stood by me, raised our children when I was off preaching somewhere, and believed in what I was doing.

My children also believed in what I was doing. I can't remember one time my daughters ever said, "Daddy, we wish you weren't a preacher. We wish you were like other fathers and were here more for us."

I remember one time when I came home Jerriann and Terri said, "Daddy, we want you to know while you were gone this time, we gave you away."

"What do you mean, you gave me away?"

They said, "We know you're called to preach to people, so we gave you to the world and we're believing for a return."

"Not for a different daddy?"

"No, we're believing that someday we'll have more time with you. But you go ahead and preach to the world, because we've given you to the world."

I can't express in words what it's like to have a wife and daughters who believe in me this way. My heart is full as I look at my two girls now. They are both beautiful women with their own families and their own ministries and are preaching the Word of God.

Carolyn and I trust our conversation has been a blessing to you as we've shared some of the more intimate times with the people who made such an impact on our lives.

God bless you, and we pray from this moment forward that your ministry will continue to grow as you stay true to your vision, that you will increase in the anointing of God, and that if you're married, your love for each other will continue to grow beyond your wildest imaginations.